MW01142922

PRENTICE HALL

Language Teaching Methodology Series

Classroom Techniques and Resources

General Editor: Christopher N. Candlin

Vocabulary in Action

Other titles in this series include:

ARGONDIZZO, Carmen
Children in action

DORNYEI, Zoltan and THURRELL, Sarah
Conversation and dialogues in action

FRANK, Christine and RINVOLUCRI, Mario
Grammar in action again

GERNGROSS, Gunter and PUCHTA, Herbert
Pictures in action

GOLEBIOWSKA, Aleksandra
Getting students to talk

GRIFFEE, Dale
Songs in action

McKAY, Sandra
Teaching grammar

NUNAN, David
Language teaching methodology

NUNAN, David
Understanding language classrooms

PECK, Antony
Language teachers at work

ROST, Michael
Listening in action

STEMPLESKI, Susan and TOMALIN, Barry
Video in action

STEVICK, Earl
Success with foreign languages

TAYLOR, Linda
Teaching and learning vocabulary

WINGATE, Jim
Getting beginners to talk

YALDEN, Janice
The communicative syllabus

Vocabulary in Action

LINDA TAYLOR

ENGLISH LANGUAGE TEACHING

Prentice Hall
New York London Toronto Sydney Tokyo Singapore

First published 1992 by
Prentice Hall International
Campus 400, Spring Way
Maylands Avenue, Hemel Hempstead
Hertfordshire, HP2 7EZ

© International Book Distributors Ltd

All rights reserved. No reproduction, copy or transmission of this publication may be made without written permission or in accordance with the provisions of the Copyright, Designs and Patents Act 1988, or under the terms of any licence permitting limited copying issued by the Copyright Licensing Agency, 90 Tottenham court Road, London, W1P 9HE

Typeset in 10½/12½pt Times
by MHL Typesetting Ltd, Coventry

Printed and bound in Great Britain

Library of Congress Cataloging-in-Publication Data

Taylor, Linda (Linda L.)
Vocabulary in action / Linda Taylor.
p. cm. -- (English language teaching)
Includes bibliographical references and index.
ISBN 0-13-950916-X
1. Vocabulary. I. Title. II. Series.
PE1449.T37 1992
428.1--dc20 91-30856
CIP

British Library Cataloguing in Publication Data

Taylor, Linda
Vocabulary in action. — (Language teaching methodology series)
I. Title II. Series
428

ISBN 0-13-950916-X

---

3 4 5 96 95

Contents

Preface

With the Language Teaching Methodology Series we have created a special set of books with the *In Action* title. These books are designed to offer teachers material that can be directly used in class. They are resources for action, hence the title. They offer language teachers material which can be adapted with various inputs for their own classroom work. The activities are presented in an accessible and teacher-friendly way, with a clear identification of teacher and learner roles, and above all, they consist of tried and tested tasks. The authors of the books in the *In Action* collection all have considerable practical experience of teaching and of classroom research. It is this combination of principle and practice, available in an easily accessible form for the teacher, which characterises the design of the books. We hope that they will not only help teachers to plan and carry out exciting lessons but also to develop themselves as reflective teachers by suggesting action research that can be done with their own learners.

There is a probably apocryphal story that when asked whether he would prefer to be marooned on a desert island with only one book, a grammar or a dictionary, a famous linguist opted quite clearly for the dictionary. It is not difficult to see why. Only the dictionary would have provided insights into not only the structure and form of the language but also in its subject-matter, its cultural content and its social world. Vocabulary has that all-encompassing linguistic character. It offers ways into understanding how the language constructs its grammar, how it conceives of its metaphors, how it organises and frames its world and how its speakers and writers are enabled to transmit with precision what they want to convey. It is no wonder, then, that teachers have made vocabulary one of the key components of their curriculum, even if from time to time it seems to take second place to grammar.

Linda Taylor follows up her recent book on vocabulary in the Teacher Education sub-series of the *Prentice Hall Language Teaching Methodology Series* with this specially designed classroom resource book for teachers. *Vocabulary in Action* highlights the grammatical, semantic and pragmatic aspects of vocabulary, showing through its lively activities how classrooms can explore not only the structure of words but how they connect and collocate, how they are classified into various registers and sets, how we continually define and redefine the meanings of words in our speech and in our writing. Like the other books in the *In Action* collection, the activities are classified according to a range of criteria, including here the structure of vocabulary, the links between vocabulary teaching and the development of language learning strategies, the use of vocabulary in reading, writing, listening and speaking and, especially, how vocabulary teaching can be made a central part of the whole language learning curriculum. Readers will find her references and indexes extremely valuable and the suggestions for action research will make it possible for the class not only to learn about vocabulary but actively to explore how it is structured and how it develops and changes. Above all, she shows how the study of words and their meanings can be both enjoyable and instructive, allowing learners to make the connections between language structure and language context.

As General Editor, I hope that the books in this new *In Action* collection will continue the success of the *Language Teaching Methodology Series* more generally in developing the skills and knowledge of the reflective language teacher in the classroom.

Professor Christopher N. Candlin
General Editor

Acknowledgements

I should like to thank David Haines and Isobel Fletcher de Téllez for their friendship, advice and support during the production of this book. I should also like to thank the many colleagues and trainees with whom I have worked, and who have provided the impetus for this collection of ideas, in particular:

Bok Hei, Hyang Hei and Lee Goodwin
Esra Bozyazi
Tristy Taylor
Liz Mason
Ted Wild
Peter Winfield
Tom Moffat
Jose Carlos
Sandie Spanton
Peter Harmer
Greg White
Paul Sutton
Kyoko Nitta

Thanks are due to the following: Pan Books, for permission to print the illustration from J. Farman, *You Can't Tell a Rook by Its Cover*, 1989, on p. 25; Open University Publications for permission to print an extract from Gaby Weiner, ed., *Just a Bunch of Girls*, 1985, on p. 89; Collins, for permission to print the frequency list on p. 107; BBC Broadcasting, for permission to use material from the show 'Blankety Blank', on p. 112, and for permission to print the transcript from 'Science Now', on p. 176; Crest Hotels plc, Gore-Tex and Dulux, for permission to print the advertisements on p. 125; the *Retford and Bawtry Trader*, *Retford Times*, the *Guardian* newspaper and the Readers Digest Association Ltd, for permission to print the material on pp. 140–1; A.P. Watt Limited on behalf of The Trustees of the Robert Graves Copyright Trust for permission to print the poem, 'It was all very tidy' by Robert Graves, on p. 141, quoted from *Collected Poems*, 1975.

L.T.

INTRODUCTION

Structure and content

Vocabulary in Action is a book of vocabulary-related teaching ideas. Vocabulary permeates everything we do in an English language class, whichever skill or language point is being practised. This book explores eleven different aspects of 'knowledge of a word', and is divided into sections which correspond to these. Within each section there is a choice of activities designed to provide work focused on the chosen aspect. A short introduction at the beignning of each of these sections explains the rationale behind the exercises concerned and gives an overall view of their content. The eleven aspects dealt with in this book are:

Mother tongue equivalence

This is knowledge of the equivalent of the vocabulary item in the mother tongue. Bilingual dictionaries are in constant use and, although many teachers discourage speaking in the mother tongue in class, it can be valuable to discuss and compare how things are said in different languages. To banish the mother tongue in the classroom would be to diminish its status, and, in any case, translation is bound to occur among students, especially in monolingual groups. There will always be items in the target language which have a similar sound to those in the mother tongue, sometimes humorously so. Translation can aid understanding, especially where there are 'false friends'. It also has a role to play in raising cultural awareness.

Sound–spelling

There is no simple one-to-one relationship between the letters of the English alphabet and the way they are pronounced. Many words sound identical though they are spelled differently, and vice versa, so that it is important for teachers to attend to the relationship of sound and spelling. When they encounter a new word, elementary learners pay more attention to the way it sounds than to what it means. They do understand meaning but appear to encode words in memory on the basis of sound and spelling. As they become more proficient, strategies of encoding vocabulary in memory change. One helpful suggestion, especially for elementary learners, is for the teacher to set new items into the context of other known words of similar spelling or sound, e.g. 'mane', 'name', 'mean'. A knowledge of the sound–spelling relationship is of particular relevance to learners unfamiliar with Roman script.

Denotation

This is the aspect most of us think of when we are asked, 'What does this word mean?' Teachers can explain this kind of meaning by bringing objects or pictures into the class, or by drawing representations on the board. Such techniques are useful for teaching denotation of concrete items like 'banana' or 'ruler', but for more abstract concepts synonyms, paraphrase or definitions may be appropriate. It is also important to teach what the word does *not* mean, so that learners are aware of its limitations.

Word grammar

This involves the underlying form of a word and the derivations that can be made from it. For example, the word 'dissatisfaction' has a common prefix denoting 'opposite' (dis-) a common noun suffix (-ion) and is derived from the verb 'satisfy'. Knowledge of word grammar also includes the identification of word classes, for which suffixes give valuable clues. For example, if learners know that the '-ion' ending is restricted to nouns, they will be able to work out how a word with that ending behaves in context.

Collocation

Knowledge of collocation involves knowing the network of associations between the given word and other words in the language. It also involves knowing which other words can stand alongside the given word in a sentence. For example, 'overtake' is a verb, transitive or intransitive, likely to be used in active voice, and followed by article plus noun or pronoun. It is moreover likely to occur in the context of transport, with items such as 'lane', 'car', 'speed'. Idioms and fixed expressions are a great source of difficulty for foreign learners because of their strong collocations, and because there are no hard and fast rules by which they can be learned.

Polysemy

Knowledge of polysemy is knowing many of the different meanings associated with a word. For example, 'branch' can refer to part of a tree, or to a particular store which is a member of a larger network of stores. Learners are often confused when they encounter a familiar word in an unfamiliar context, or when they encounter a familiar word which is fulfilling an unfamiliar function, e.g. a noun acting as an adjective.

Frequency

Knowledge of the frequency of the word in the language is knowing the likelihood of encountering the word in speech or in print. Some items in English are far more frequent in speech than in writing — 'indeed', 'well', 'actually', for example. Others may occur only in the written language. Certain items may have high frequency for particular learners in terms of their careers or interests, so it can be motivating for them to be given the chance to decide which words they want to learn.

Connotation

This aspect of knowledge of a word gives an extra dimension to its literal meaning. It is often culture-specific: for example, in Western culture the word 'slim' is positively evaluated, but we have many euphemisms for the negatively evaluated term, 'fat', such as 'portly' 'plump' or 'well-built'. However, elsewhere in the world, 'You've put on weight' may be seen as a compliment. Many words have connotations relating to oppositions such as male/female, negative/positive, animate/inaminate, e.g. 'blouse' can refer only to a garment worn by women, even though men may wear exactly the same garment, when it is called a 'shirt'. Hidden, more personal, connotations may also exist.

Register

This refers to the appropriate use of a vocabulary item. For example, 'Would you like a cigarette?' is a neutral formula, appropriate in most contexts. 'Want a fag?' would be acceptable only between friends.

Vocabulary within written discourse

This embraces study skills and involves reference, linking, sequencing, and deciphering the meaning of unknown vocabulary items in context. It is concerned with the behaviour of words across sentence boundaries, and not with isolated words or phrases.

Vocabulary within spoken discourse

This is concerned with intonation, stress and pausing, and with the words speakers use to signal the beginnings and endings of sections of discourse. Many of the words heard in conversation have little semantic content: they keep the conversation going by maintaining interaction between speaker and hearer. For learners who are unfamiliar with spoken English it is often not the 'difficult' vocabulary which poses problems, but 'easy' little words used in unfamiliar ways.

The book has been designed so that there is a progression from decontextualised vocabulary activities towards work on vocabulary within discourse. Since elementary learners pay more attention to sound than meaning as well as relying more heavily on translation, it is the Mother Tongue Equivalence and Sound–Spelling sections which appear first. The more straightforward concepts of Denotation and Word Grammar follow. More complex ones, such as Connotation and Register require a greater level of competence, and appear later in the sequence of activities. The book ends with two Vocabulary within Discourse sections, dealing with words in context.

Methodology

The activities in this book provide individual work, but also encourage the pooling of ideas among learners by means of group and pair work, as well as whole class discussion. At the core of the book is a belief in using authentic material wherever possible, and, to this end, authentic English texts are given as material for the activities, with native speaker responses where appropriate. Another concept fundamental to this book is the belief that learners cannot concentrate both on 'surface form' and 'meaning content' at once; therefore, some activities focus on spelling or word formation, while others focus on comprehension. Most follow the format below:

1. *Sensitisation*: A period of talking around the topic, introducing in a general way what is to be covered. Often, this part involves brainstorming.
2. *Task*: An individual, pair or group task. Sample teaching materials are provided for this.
3. *Feedback*: A coming together to pool ideas and report on what went on during the task.
4. *Analysis and follow-up*: An answer sheet or native speaker response is given for discussion. Further activity may be proposed.
5. *Reflection*: Space is given for teachers to note their impressions of how the activity progressed. Learners might also like to do this.

In order to make the best use of *Vocabulary in Action*, you should read through the introduction to each section first. You will then be in a position to know which sections and which activities will suit your learners best. The Index will also help you to locate suitable activities: it gives summaries of each activity in the book. In addition, you will find the Links Section useful: this shows other activities which are suitable as warm-ups or follow-ups to the one given. As a general rule, the sequence of activities in each section progresses from lower level/younger learners to higher level/adult learners. There is a 'Teacher's Diary' space at the end of each activity, for your comments on the response of your learners, on useful aspects of the activity, and on the revisions you would make for future sessions. Each individual activity is prefaced by an indication as to its target level, age and purpose. Detailed steps are given to teachers for both preparation and execution of the activity.

Further reading

A complete list of references appears at the end of this book. Below is a shorter list of books which I have found useful when compiling this work, and which I would recommend as further reading. The list is not meant to be exhaustive, but it is respresentative of the range of material available.

Teachers' books

Carter, R. and McCarthy, M., *Vocabulary and Language Teaching*, Harlow: Longman, 1988.

This is a collection of articles on aspects of vocabulary teaching and on dictionaries in language learning. It has a useful survey of developments in vocabulary teaching from 1945 to the present.

McCarthy, M., *Vocabulary*, Oxford: Oxford University Press, 1990.

This gives an overview of vocabulary, in language teaching and in language generally. It falls into two sections: the first giving an explanation of various theories of how the lexicon is organised, the second giving detailed illustration of how theory has been applied in teaching and reference materials.

Gairns, R. and Redman, S., *Working with Words*, Cambridge: Cambridge University Press, 1986.

This gives full and detailed explanations of several aspects of word study, with plenty of illustrative material showing what can be done to exploit these in class.

Ilson, R. (ed.), *Dictionaries, Lexicography and Language Learning*, ELT Documents 120, British Council, Oxford: Pergamon Press, 1985

This is a collection of essays by lexicographers, linguists, and language teachers on the subject of English language learners' dictionaries, their content and their use. The article on working with monolingual learners' dictionaries is of direct usefulness for the classroom.

Morgan, J. and Rinvolucri, M., *Vocabulary*, Oxford: Oxford University Press, 1986.

This is a wholly practical resource book to dip into, rather than to work through. It consists of vocabulary-related teaching ideas, with detailed descriptions of procedures.

Taylor, L., *Teaching and Learning Vocabulary*, Hemel Hempstead: Prentice Hall, 1990.

This is the companion work to this book. It provides a bridge between theory and practice, by linking insights gained from applied linguistics to practical activities for the classroom. It also has a discussion of vocabulary acquisition, illustrated with classroom extracts. There are two sets of reader tasks, one designed for group work and the other for self study.

Wallace, M., *Teaching Vocabulary*, 3rd edn, London: Heinemann, 1987.

This book is suitable for both pre- and in-service teachers. It is clearly laid out in sections devoted to such aspects as vocabulary acquisition and teaching vocabulary in context. It has a useful section on teaching idioms and multi-word verbs.

Willis, D., *The Lexical Syllabus*, Collins ELT, London and Glasgow: Collins, 1990.

A fascinating account of a project based on important research findings, and on the pioneering Collins Cobuild English Course which draws on these findings, this book describes what a lexical syllabus is, how it can be organised, and how it can be taught within a communicative framework.

Students' books

1. Workbooks (graded)

Flower, J. and Berman, M., *Build Your Vocabulary*, Hove: Language Teaching Publications, 1988.

A series of three graded students' workbooks, each containing over sixty short exercises with key and wordlist. A useful and flexible resource book to dip into. The presentation is lively and the exercise types very varied.

Redman, S. and Ellis, R., *A Way with Words*, Cambridge: Cambridge University Press, 1991.

A series of three graded workbooks at intermediate level, with teachers' book and cassette. Self Study Activity Sections are provided at the end of each topic-based unit. Of particular note are the activities which explore how vocabulary works in discourse, and those which teach students strategies for learning vocabulary.

Seal, B., *Vocabulary Builder*, Harlow: Longman, 1988.

A series of three graded workbooks with key, which can be used for self study but are more useful as class texts. A useful feature is the inclusion of vocabulary reviews and tests at intervals throughout the books.

2. Reference and practice books

Crow, J.T., *Vocabulary for Advanced Reading Comprehension — The Key Word Approach*, Hemel Hempstead: Prentice Hall.

Of particular use for learners of ESP, this book has texts on sociology, anthropology and history among other specialised areas, followed by exercises which focus on key words from the texts.

Fowler, W.S., *The Right Word*, Nelson.

For students of intermediate to upper intermediate level, this book has topic-based units which include a range of practice exercises. Part A covers nouns and Part B covers verbs.

Harrison, M., *Word Perfect*, Nelson.

For intermediate and advanced learners, this book comprises fifty units grouped together in sections. Grammatical information and examples of usage are followed by practice exercises, in the style of Cambridge examinations, which can be worked and marked by learners themselves, using the word list and key.

Farid, A., *A Vocabulary Workbook*, Hemel Hempstead: Prentice Hall, 1985.

For upper intermediate and advanced learners, this book focuses on prefixes, roots and suffixes. There is a wordlist and key, making it suitable for self study.

Wellman, G., *The Heinemann English Wordbuilder*, London: Heinemann, 1989.

Packed with information and with a lively presentation, this is a substantial work which will be appreciated by students working for Cambridge examinations up to Proficiency level, and by ESP students. There is a huge variety of exercise types to accompany the study texts. There is a key and full wordlist at the back, so it can be used for self study, though students will gain much from working through the communicative tasks in class.

3. Picture books and puzzle books

Sanabria, D., *A Picture's Worth a Thousand Words*, Hemel Hempstead: Prentice Hall, 1988.

Suitable for children at elementary and intermediate level, this book is full of picture-based exercises which are motivating and fun.

Howard-Williams, D. and Herd, C., *Word Games with English* and *Word Games with English Plus*, London: Heinemann, 1989.

A series of little books of games and puzzles designed to stimulate learners to practise and extend their English vocabulary. The answers are in the key at the back, so learners can work through the book alone, but teachers will find it a source of lively and motivating material for lesson fillers or homework tasks.

4. Dictionary workbooks

There is a range available, of which the *Heinemann Picture Dictionary Skills Book*, Oxford: Heinemann, 1986, for children at elementary level, and *Learning Real English with Collins Cobuild English Language Dictionary*, 1987, for adults up to advanced level, are at opposite ends of the spectrum.

SECTION I

MOTHER TONGUE EQUIVALENCE

Introduction

There are six activities in this section:

1. **Marks on a paper**
2. **Key words**
3. **What did you call me?**
4. **Sound feelings**
5. **Borrowings**
6. **Word-for-word translation**

This section deals with vocabulary items as 'signs'. It concerns itself with knowledge of the infinitely variable written and spoken forms of the world's languages. The first four activities are very simple in that they involve learners in producing only single words or sounds. Activity 5 moves to a problem-solving task matching items of vocabulary with their language of origin. Activity 6 compares fixed expressions in various languages. While the first five activities are suitable for all levels of ability, the final one is for learners of intermediate level or above. All the activities in this section would integrate very well into topic work on the nature of language or of the world's languages, and they could also serve as 'ice breakers' for use at the beginning of a course, when learners are getting to know each other.

1 Marks on a paper

Level Elementary to advanced, especially mixed-nationality groups

Students All ages

Groups Individual, pairs, groups, or whole class

Purpose Cultural awareness and appreciation of the richness of variety in the world's languages and of the role of translation

Text type Learner-generated wordlists

In this activity . . .

Learners look at vocabulary items written in various languages, and guess meanings.

Preparation

None at all if your class is a multilingual one. If not, use the teaching material for this activity, or find examples of your own of vocabulary from various languages.

In class

1. Ask your learners, individually, to write down the first three words which come into their head in their mother tongue.
2. Ask each learner to exchange papers with another learner who does not speak their language. They look at the unfamiliar words and try to think of a meaning for them. Decisions may be based on the shape of the word, its resemblance to other known words in whatever language, etc.
3. As a whole class activity invite a few learners to write their words on the board and explain the meanings. As they do so, other class members can note the direction of the writing, the way the pen is lifted and moved during writing, the presence or otherwise of marks like accents, the shape of the word, etc.

Follow-up

Compile a complete list of learners' words for circulation to the class. If there is enough interest, research assignments can be given for learners to find out a little about another language and to feed back information to the whole class.

Link

Sound feelings (4), in this section, has learners speak words rather than write them, and complements this activity.

Teacher's diary

How did your learners react to this activity?
What did you learn about your learners' language(s) through doing this activity?
What changes would you make for next time?

2 Key words

Level Elementary to advanced

Students All ages but especially adults

Groups Whole class

Purpose To help learners remember new vocabulary by using visual images

Text type Teacher's examples and student-generated examples

In this activity . . .

Learners make visual, auditory, or other associations to help them remember word meanings.

Preparation

Make a few flash cards of your own of examples like the one given in the teaching material for this activity.

In class

1. Ask your learners how they remember the English for some of the words in their language. Do they 'see' the written word on the page? Do they 'hear' the word as spoken on a tape they have heard? Do they 'feel' the sensation of a word, e.g. 'sun' makes them feel warm?

2. Show your learners the flash cards you have made, and ask them to volunteer their own examples: two Japanese students of mine associated each new adjective they met in their studies with one of their teachers.

Link

This activity works well as a warm up to **Kelly's eye view (33)** or **Positive/negative (36)** from the Connotation section.

Teacher's diary

How did the students react to this activity?
Which new ways of making associations emerged?

Sample teaching material

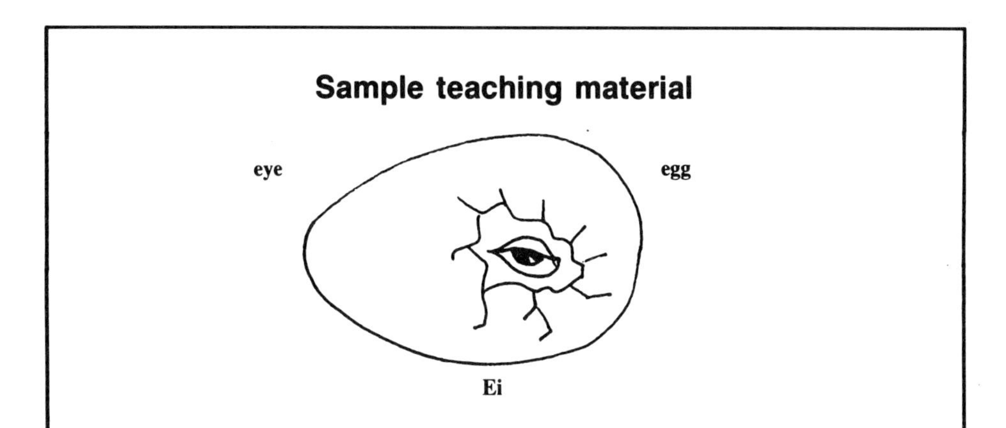

3 What did you call me?

Level	Elementary to advanced
Students	Teenage to adult
Groups	Groups and whole class
Purpose	To alert learners to some of the connotations of animal names in English
Text type	Teacher's animal words and students' own words

In this activity

Learners discuss animal names and how they are used to describe humans.

Preparation

None. A sample word list is given in the material for this activity.

In class

1. Show your learners a list of animal names in English and invite them to work in groups to decide whether they would be pleased or offended to be called by each name.
2. As a whole class activity, pool ideas from the groups before giving the Key (in the material for this activity).
3. Ask your learners to share with each other the significance of animal names in their mother tongues. How do they differ? Are some animal names used as terms of endearment? ('mon lapin' in French would be rendered by 'dove' rather than 'rabbit' in English).

Link

Positive/negative (36) makes a good follow-up activity to this one, from the Connotation section.

Teacher's diary

How did the students react to this activity? What did you learn about your students' perceptions of the relative strength of animal words, in English and in their own language(s)? Would you change anything for next time?

Sample teaching material

Wordlist:

1. Ass
2. Bitch
3. Chicken
4. Cow
5. Goose
6. Monkey
7. Pig
8. Rat

Native speaker key:

1. Stupid person (mild)
2. Vindictive female (strong)
3. Coward (fairly strong)
4. Spiteful female (strong)
5. Acts without thinking (mild)
6. Cheeky (very mild)
7. Uncouth (strong)
8. Not to be trusted (strong)

4 Sound feelings

Level	Elementary to advanced, especially mixed-nationality groups
Students	All ages
Groups	Whole class
Purpose	To sensitise learners to the sound of other languages and to their own prejudices about it
Text type	Learners' own words/phrases

In this activity

Learners explore their reactions to sounds of different languages.

Preparation

None, if you have a mixed-nationality class. If not, you will need to make a tape recording of words and phrases spoken in several languages.

In class

1. Invite your learners, individually, to say a word or phrase in their mother tongue, or in a language they speak which is not English. The other learners listen and note how they feel about each word or phrase and what they think it means.
2. Ask learners to share their individual reactions with the whole class, and to hear the true meaning and use of the words they have been discussing. Distribute copies of the material for this activity if appropriate.

Follow-up

Go on to discuss which English sounds are agreeable or not to the ear, with examples elicited from learners.

Link

This activity leads on to work on Connotation, such as **Positive/negative (36)** from that section.

Teacher's diary

How did the learners react to this activity? What did you learn about their prejudices and perceptions?

Sample teaching material

Learner comment:

'I find the French language, erm, very melodic to listen to. It's very easy on the ear, erm, and it almost sounds poetic, er, no matter what kind of mood the individual is in who's talking, or what they're talking about, there seems to be a rhythm to the language.'

5 Borrowings

Level Elementary to advanced

Students Teenage to adult

Groups Groups or whole class

Purpose To sensitise learners to the richness of borrowings from other languages into English

Text type Teacher's word lists

In this activity

Learners explore some of the words which English has borrowed from other languages and vice versa, through a matching exercise.

Preparation

Assemble your own list of borrowings, or use the sample material for this activity.

In class

1. Ask your learners whether they know of any English words which are used in their own language. Write them on the board — some may be used in other languages too.
2. Ask your learners if they know any words from their own language which are used in English. Write these up too.
3. Distribute copies of the sample jumbled wordlist exercise for this activity. Have your learners match the words in List A with their corresponding country of origin from List B for Exercise 1, and with their corresponding language of origin in List B for Exercise 2.

Follow-up

Discuss with your learners which sounds they think are peculiarly English, e.g. consonant clusters.

Link

Activities from the Sound–Spelling section, particularly **How do I say it? (11)** would lead on from this one.

Teacher's diary

How did the learners react to this activity? What did you learn about English words borrowed into your students' own language(s)? Would you change any aspect of the activity for next time?

Sample teaching material

Exercise 1

List A:

1. Window, husband, skin, ugly
2. Government, parliament, palace, nation
3. Piano, soprano, macaroni, violin
4. Skipper, yacht, deck, tattoo
5. Bungalow, calico, chintz, pyjamas

List B:

1. Italy
2. Scandinavia
3. Holland
4. France
5. India

Exercise 2

List A:

robot, silk, sputnik, coach, yoghurt, flak, ketchup, boomerang, cigar, mohair

List B:

Russian, Turkish, Chinese, German, Czech, Hungarian, Arabic, Malay, Spanish, Australian

6 Word-for-word translation

Level	Intermediate to advanced, especially mixed-nationality group
Students	Teenage to adult
Groups	Whole class
Purpose	To raise cultural awareness in respect of differences in expressing the same overall idea (- idioms)
Text type	Learner-generated, prompted by teacher's examples

In this activity

Learners compare proverbs from their language with their equivalents in English.

Preparation

None. The sample material for this activity gives proverbs which translate into several languages, and may be useful.

In class

1. Tell your learners a few English proverbs, e.g.: 'A bird in the hand is worth two in the bush'; 'Better late than never', etc.

2. Invite your learners to volunteer proverbs from their own language and to explain them in English. If these proverbs are translated word for word, are they recognisable? Do they perhaps express the same overall idea, but with different collocations, e.g. 'I haven't any bread' is rendered in German by the equivalent of 'I haven't any coal', to mean that the speaker has no cash.

3. Compile a list for the class to keep of the proverbs they have volunteered, perhaps including the samples in the material given for this activity.

Link

This activity leads quite naturally into one on idoms, such as **Variations on a theme (24)** from the Collocation section.

Teacher's diary

How did the students react to this activity? Did you learn any new proverbs? What would you change in the procedure for next time?

Sample teaching material

One man's meat is another man's poisson

1. English: Beggars can't be choosers
   Italian: Eat this soup or jump out of the window
2. English: A woman's work is never done
   Japanese: A poor man can't have free time

3.	English:	As bald as a coot
	French:	As bald as an egg
	Spanish:	As bald as a billiard ball
	Japanese:	As bald as a kettle/kettlehead
4.	English:	A bird in the hand is worth two in the bush
	French:	One 'Here you are' is worth more than two 'You'll have it's
	Spanish:	Better a bird in the hand than twenty on the wing
	Italian:	Better an egg today than a hen tomorrow
5.	English:	Jack of all trades, master of none
	Japanese:	The man who chases two rabbits can't catch one
6.	English:	Every cloud has a silver lining
	Japanese:	There's no night without dawn

SECTION II

SOUND – SPELLING

Introduction

There are five activities in this section:

7. **Form-focused spelling puzzles**
8. **Syllable snap and rhyming snap**
9. **Sneaky spelling practice**
10. **Colour-coded sounds**
11. **How do I say it?**

Every learner who needs to read or write in English has to come to grips with English spelling, in which a single sound can often be represented in many ways. There is no easy way to master this except by writing, listening, and speaking aloud new vocabulary items. Copying exercises and dictations may be tried, but learners often find the former too mechanical, and the latter too difficult. The activities presented here attempt to make spelling fun. In Activity 7, the learners concentrate on word forms by completing a crossword or wordsearch, and solving anagrams whose answers are thematically linked. Activity 8 uses a game format to practise phonics. Activity 9 gives several gamelike ideas for painless spelling practice. Activity 10 is a set of sound discrimination exercises adapted from a Silent Way technique linking sounds with colours, and Activity 11 uses rhyme for sensitising learners to the way vowel sounds are spelled. The first four activities are applicable to students of all ages, whereas the final one is more suitable for adults of intermediate level and above who enjoy analysis. None of the activities involves learners in producing much more than single words, so that most will feel confident doing the tasks. All the activities are form-focused, except for Activity 9, in which learners are more concerned with the problem-solving process than with the language product as such.

7 Form-focused spelling puzzles

Level	Elementary to advanced
Students	All ages
Groups	Individual, pair or group
Purpose	To focus on the spelling of words for review
Text type	Teacher's word puzzle

In this activity

Learners focus on the correct ordering of letters within a given word, and on the correspondence between letters and sounds.

Preparation

Prepare a crossword, wordsearch or anagram set having a thematic link. Samples are given in the teaching material for this activity:

Crosswords: provide clues as usual, but link the words in the crossword via a common theme, e.g. a sound or a prefix, as in the sample.

Wordsearch: provide a list of words to be found which is linked in some way, or give a clue to the lexical set involved, e.g. 'days of the week'.

Anagrams: provide some kind of unifying theme for your anagrams, e.g. by using letters which can form several words, or by using visuals, as in the sample.

In class

1. Invite your learners to work in pairs or groups, or individually, to solve the word puzzles.
2. Bring the whole class together to report on their solutions. It is important that

individuals should speak answers aloud, so that the sound—spelling relationship can be fully appreciated and discussed.

Link

English as she is spoke (50) from the Vocabulary within Spoken Discourse section, would be a good follow-up activity to this.

Teacher's diary

Did your learners enjoy this activity? Did it lead to greater facility with spelling? Would you change any of the procedures next time?

Sample teaching material

1. Crossword: All the answers have one consonant sound in common

Clues Across:

1. Very large person
2. Liquid made from fruit
6. Heirs

Clues Down:

1. Kind and caring
4. Earth science
5. Person of no fixed address

				[1]G	I	A	N	T
[2]J	U	I	C	E				
		[3]D	A	N	[4]G	E	R	
	L	I	T	T	E	R		[5]G
		O		L	O	R	R	Y
		T		E	L	F		P
					O			S
		[6]P	R	O	G	E	N	Y
					Y			

2. Wordsearch: Find six days of the week. Which one is missing?

E	O	N	W	T	H	U
F	R	I	E	N	U	S
F	R	I	D	A	Y	A
S	M	O	N	D	A	Y
A	S	M	E	I	D	O
T	U	E	S	D	A	Y
U	N	A	D	O	I	M
R	O	S	A	A	U	O
D	A	U	Y	M	Y	N
A	Y	N	A	O	T	D
Y	I	D	D	N	U	A

3. Anagrams: How many English words can you find for:

ENMA ETAM ALED LAFO

and what are the words portrayed by the pictures?

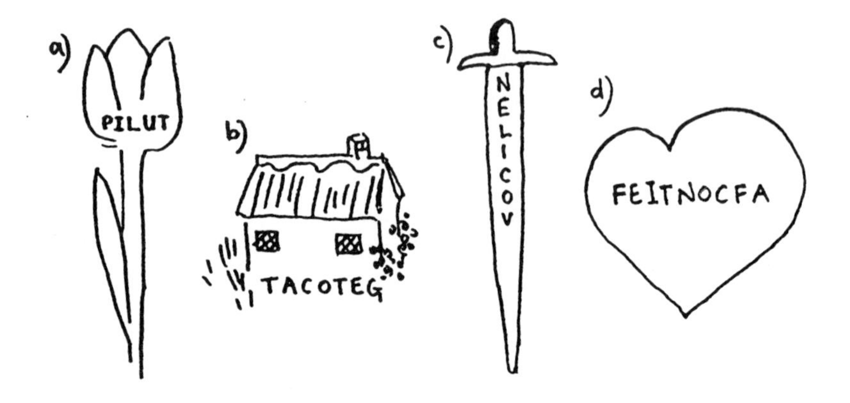

8 Syllable snap and rhyming snap

Level	Elementary to advanced, depending on input
Students	Children
Groups	Groups
Purpose	To focus on the sound and rhythm of English words
Text type	Teacher's word cards

In this activity

Learners find words with similar vowel sounds or with equal numbers of syllables.

Preparation

Make your own rhyming or syllable cards using words your learners have met, or use the sample teaching material for this activity. You will need sets of identical cards if groups are to play simultaneously.

In class

Rhyming snap:

1. Write on the board the words 'mane', 'rain', and 'mine' and ask your learners to say which two rhyme. Ask for other rhymes, e.g. 'train', 'pain', 'cane'.
2. Demonstrate the game with one group of learners, watched by the rest of the class: Deal an equal number of cards to each person, face-down. Learners should not look at their cards. The first player takes his top card and places it face-up in the middle of the table. The next player places his top card face-up on top of the first player's card. Hold these two up for the rest of the class to see. If these two cards rhyme, player No. 2 says 'snap' and takes all the cards. If the cards do not rhyme, they remain in the middle of the table. In either case, the turn passes to the next player, and the game continues until one player holds all the cards.
3. Give out identical packs to groups of learners and allow them to play, while you monitor what is going on, checking 'snaps' and giving advice where needed.

Syllable snap:

The sample material is for younger learners and uses animal names, but words need not be linked thematically:

1. Write on the board the words 'rhinoceros', 'elephant' and 'kangaroo' and ask your learners to say which have the same number of syllables. Ask for other animal names having three syllables, e.g. 'flamingo', 'okapi'.
2. Demonstrate the game, rules as for rhyming snap above.
3. Give out identical packs of cards to groups of learners and proceed as with rhyming snap above.

Link

This activity could lead on to **English as she is spoke (50)** in the Vocabulary within Spoken Discourse section.

Teacher's diary

How did the learners react to this activity? Did you think that learners were being made aware of sound–spelling relationships by doing this activity? Would you change anything in the procedure for next time?

Sample teaching material

Rhyming snap:

MANE	RAIN	MINE	TRAIN	PAIN	CANE
SIGN	LANE	FINE	LINE	MEET	EAT
SHEET	CHEAT	MATE	PLATE	GREAT	FATE
SOON	TUNE	MOON	PRUNE	USE	LOSE
LOOSE	NOOSE	NEWS	WHOSE		

Syllable snap:

TIGER	ELEPHANT	KANGAROO	FLAMINGO	APE	MONKEY
PENGUIN	OKAPI	BISON	BEAR	CAMEL	GIRAFFE
OTTER	HAMSTER	MOUSE	CHEETAH	SNAKE	RHINOCEROS
OWL	OSTRICH	ANTELOPE	SEAL	GORILLA	ORANGOUTAN

9 Sneaky spelling practice

Level	Elementary to advanced
Students	All ages
Groups	Individual, group or whole class
Purpose	To provide spelling practice through problem-solving
Text type	Teacher's visual cards, incomplete pictures, quiz, diagram or text

In this activity

Learners engage in acquisition-based spelling.

In order to practise spelling, learners need to write and rewrite the target word correctly. For those who are easily bored by such mechanical tasks, here are a few ways of focusing on spelling without seeming to:

Variation 1: Kim's game

Preparation

Assemble a tray of small objects whose spelling you wish to review.

In class

Show the learners your tray of objects, then cover over the tray and ask learners to write down as many of the objects as they can remember. The winner is the one with the most correctly named — and spelled — items.

Variation 2: Incomplete pictures

Preparation

Draw or cut out a set of incomplete pictures, i.e. having a missing feature such as a chimney missing from a house roof.

In class

Show your picture set to the class and invite learners to write down what is missing. This can be done individually, or as a team game, with the winner having most correctly spelled items.

Variation 3: Dictionary quiz

Preparation

Choose a letter page from the class dictionary and make a quiz based on it, e.g. for 'f' words, 'something healthy, juicy and sweet to eat' could be a clue for the word 'fruit'.

In class

Give out copies of your quiz either to individuals or groups. You could give a small prize to the first to complete the quiz successfully.

Variation 4: Labelling a diagram

Preparation

Prepare a text with accompanying diagram for completion but provide a twist in the procedure, e.g. learners have a problem to solve before they can find out the label names, only some of the names from the text have to be labelled on the diagram, or learners must provide their own labels.

In class

Present your chosen text and diagram to individuals, pairs or groups. After a suitable time spent on the task, bring the class together for feedback and pooling of answers.

Variation 5: List-writing competitions

Preparation

None.

In class

Ask your learners to write down the first five things they would take with them to a desert island/camping trip/seaside holiday, etc. When everyone has five words, ask one learner to read out a word from their list and to score a point if it is spelled correctly. Everyone else who has written that word (correctly) scores a point too. Four more learners then read out one of their words, which is scored in the same way. Add up the marks awarded and declare the winner.

Link

These are all game-like activities. Other similar activities are **The definition game (12)** in the Denotation section, and **The affix game (21)** and **Add to it (20)** from the Word Grammar section.

Teacher's diary

Which activities did you try? What was the reaction of the learners? Did you notice any particular spelling problems which might need further work? Would you change anything in the procedure for next time?

10 Colour-coded sounds

Level Elementary to advanced

Students All ages

Groups Whole class and individual

Purpose To use colour as a trigger for memorising sounds normally confused or mispronounced

Text type Teacher's wordlist and coloured card

In this activity

Learners associate problem sounds with particular colours in order to improve sound discrimination.

Preparation

Colour charts are an integral part of the Silent Way of teaching languages. This activity uses colour to form an association in your learners' minds between a colour and a sound. If you want to try all three variations given below, you will need coloured cards in seven separate colours to match the seven sounds given in the sample material for this activity. It does not matter which colours you choose, so long as they are easily distinguishable from each other.

In class

1. Present your chosen sounds in connection with the colours you have chosen for them, i.e. hold up the /t/ card, say a word containing the sound /t/, such as 'tin' and elicit other /t/ words from your learners, then proceed to the next card, and so on. As you finish with each card, put it on the board. In this way, you should end up with seven cards on the board if you are using all the given sounds.

2. Now take a pointer and point to a succession of cards, so as to form an English word, e.g. /s/ /e/ /d/ = 'said'. Invite a learner to say the sounds as you point

to them, and another learner to give the English spelling. Make other words in the same way, e.g. 'eat', 'easy', 'did', etc.

3. Finally, invite learners themselves to point out sounds for others to say. It does not matter if they make a nonsense word — just accept the sound sequence and say that there is no word in English which corresponds to it.

Variation 1: Past tenses /t/, /d/, /ɪd/

Revise the colours associated with these four sounds and post the appropriate coloured cards on the board to correspond to the three verb endings. Call out past tense forms, e.g. 'watched', 'arranged', 'decided' while individual learners at the board point to the correct colour code for the verbs you have called.

Variation 2: Plural forms /s/, /z/, /ɪz/

Revise the colours associated with these sounds and post the appropriate coloured cards on the board to correspond to the three plural endings. Call out plural forms, e.g. 'ants', 'flies', 'peaches' while individual learners at the board point to the correct colour code for the plural forms you have called.

Variation 3: Vowel discrimination /i/, /ɪ/, /e/

Revise the colours associated with these sounds and post the appropriate coloured cards on the board to correspond to these three vowel sounds. Call out words having one of the sounds, e.g. 'meet', 'pick', 'shelf', while individual learners at the board point to the correct colour code for the word you have called.

Link

Spelling puzzles such as those in **Sneaky spelling practice (9)** from the Sound–spelling section, **Hearing and visualising (15)** from the Denotation section, and **Photofits (37)** from the Register section are other activities which will appeal to visual learners.

Teacher's diary

How did the learners react to this activity? Did you notice any learners who seemed to benefit greatly from the visual associations? Would you change anything in the procedure for next time?

Sample teaching material

Seven-sound set:

<table>
<tr><td>/t/</td><td>/d/</td><td>/s/</td><td rowspan="2">/z/</td></tr>
<tr><td>/i/</td><td>/ɪ/</td><td>/e/</td></tr>
</table>

11 How do I say it?

Level Intermediate to advanced

Students Adults

Groups Pairs and groups

Purpose To use rhyme for sensitising learners to the different ways of spelling vowel sounds in English, and to accent variation in their pronunciation

Text type Teacher's wordlist

In this activity

Learners group words according to whether they sound the same or different, whether they rhyme or not, and whether they have two possible pronunciations.

Preparation

Choose an exercise from the sample material from this activity. It is graded in difficulty from Variation 1 to Variation 3.

In class 1

Variation 1:

Present List 1 and invite your learners, working in pairs or groups, to find other words which sound the same as those in the list, but are spelled differently.

Variation 2:

Present List 2 and invite your learners, working in groups, to say which can rhyme and which cannot.

Variation 3:

Present List 3 and invite your learners, working in groups, to find two ways of pronouncing each. If possible, they should interview native speakers for this, but dictionaries can be used if not.

In class 2

Bring the class together for feedback and pooling of ideas. Then give out copies of the key given in the sample material for this activity.

Link

English as she is spoke (50) in the Vocabulary within Spoken Discourse section is another activity which explores English phonology.

Teacher's diary

Which variation did you try? How did the learners react? Which sounds seemed to cause most problems? Would you change anything in the procedure for next time?

Sample teaching material

List 1:

hole	where	course	night
mayor	deer	new	pain
beech	rowed	bury	wait
here	pier	heal	write

Key:
whole/wear/coarse/knight/mare/dear/knew/pane/beach/road/berry/weight/hear/peer/heel/right

List 2:

1. cough/tough
2. bow/so
3. heard/bird
4. bare/tear
5. arithmetic/anaesthetic
6. bother/another

Key:
1. cannot rhyme 2. can rhyme
3. always rhymes in standard accent 4. can rhyme

5. does not rhyme because of stress placement if both used as nouns
6. does not rhyme except in accents other than standard

List 3:

1. either	2. again	3. ate	4. row
5. read	6. can	7. the	8. garage
9. pub	10. bath	11. wind	12. tear

Key:

1. aɪðə/iðə	2. ageɪn/agen	3. eɪt/et
4. rəʊ/rɑʊ	5. red/rɪd	6. kæn/kən
7. ði/ðə	8. gærɑʒ/gærɪdʒ	9. pʌb/pʊb
10. bɑθ/bæθ	11. wɪnd/waɪnd	12. tiə/teə

SECTION III

DENOTATION

Introduction

There are five activities in this section:

12. The definition game

13. Tools of the trade

14. Instant recognition

15. Hearing and visualising

16. Experiencing is knowing

This section is concerned with semantics: the aspect teachers deal with in the course of every lesson in answer to the question, 'What does this word mean?' Our response may be a synonym, a definition, a visual representation or an example in context. If there is no teacher at hand to explain, learners turn to their dictionaries, and so it is important for learners to understand the language of definitions. The first two activities take the function of defining as their starting point. Both of them involve learners in gamelike activities. Activity 14 is designed to familiarise learners with common phrases which they might encounter in public places. The remaining two activities in the section are based on words denoting more abstract concepts. These are less easy to teach because their meaning is often associated with personal experience. By sharing these experiences, learners become familiar with the possibilities and limitations in the use of abstract emotive words. The first three activities can be done by students of any level and especially by young learners. However, the last two require learners to appreciate the attitudes which lie behind the actual words we use, and so these activities are more appropriate for post-intermediate adult learners. The section as a whole deals with the 'content' of vocabulary rather than with its surface form, and these activities can be linked with other 'content'-based sections, i.e. Register and Connotation, and to 'content'-based activities from the Vocabulary within Discourse sections.

12 The definition game

Level	Elementary to intermediate
Students	All ages
Groups	Individual, then pairs or groups
Purpose	To enable learners to understand the language of dictionary definitions
Text type	Teacher's definitions of everyday objects, visual aids

In this activity

Learners practise defining and understanding definitions in communicative contexts.

Preparation

Assemble a number of small objects and put them together in a box, which you will take to class. Choose a few pictures of objects as prompts for revision. Write a few definitions of everyday objects, which should ideally include some of the ones in your box. Sample pictures and student definitions are given.

In class

1. Revise the structures 'It's used for . . .' and 'It's made of . . .' and language for describing objects, using the pictures you have brought. Practise them by asking learners themselves to give definitions for the objects in your pictures.
2. Show your learners your 'box of tricks' without revealing its contents. Secretly take out one of the small objects, move around behind one of your learners and put it into his hand without letting any of the others see it. Ask him to describe what he has been given. Other learners try to guess the object, and the turn passes to the one who guesses correctly. The game continues in the same way until all the objects in the box have been described.
3. Invite your learners to write their own definitions for an everyday object, which they must not name. They then swop definitions with another student and try to

guess the object defined. Sample students' definitions are given in the material for this activity.

Link

This activity is a good warm-up exercise for the game **Tools of the trade (13)** from this section.

Teacher's diary

How did your learners react to this activity? Can you think of other ways of exploiting definitions in class? Would you change anything in the procedure for next time?

Sample teaching material

Students' definitions:

1. It is made of metal or plastic. It is used for draining food. We use it twice a day in our country.
2. This is a thing you drink sometimes. It comes in different colours, but it is not pleasant.
3. It is made of glass, metal or plastic. You can find it in every class in the college. It is circular and has channels in it.

Key:
1. a colander 2. medicine 3. an ashtray

Picture set:

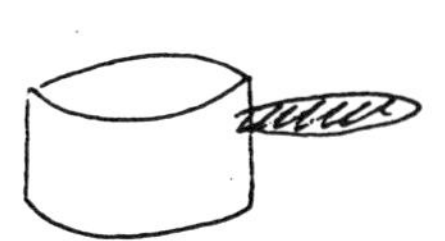

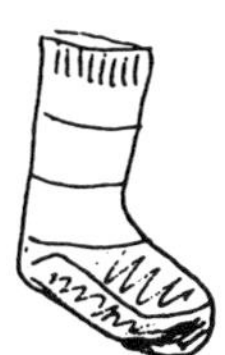

13 Tools of the trade

Level Elementary to intermediate

Students Teenage to adult

Groups Groups

Purpose To review the vocabulary of occupations and of everyday objects

Text type Teacher's occupation and object cards

In this activity

Learners engage in a communicative game involving the vocabulary for review.

Preparation

You will need a set of object picture cards, such as the one given as sample material for this activity. You will need a set of word cards, equal in number to the picture cards, on which you have written names of occupations. Sample word cards are given. Make enough copies of these two card sets so that groups of four can play the game simultaneously.

In class

1. Explain to the class the rules of the game, demonstrating with one group while the others watch: the dealer deals all the occupation cards equally among the players. The picture cards are placed face-downwards in the centre of the table. The first player picks up a picture card and tries to match it to an occupation card in her/his hand for which the pictured object would be useful. She may not have an appropriate occupation card in her hand, but she can try to make out a plausible case, e.g., if she has 'mechanic' and picks up a picture of a needle, she might say, 'A mechanic always carries a needle for removing awkward pieces of debris from places between the engine parts.' Other players decide if the reason given for matching the two cards is a good one, in which case the player can keep the pair of cards. The turn passes to the next player, and so on, the winner being the player with the most pairs when all cards have been played.

2. Divide your learners into groups of four, and give each group a set of the two types of card you have made. All groups then play the game simultaneously, while you give help where needed.

Link

This game forms a follow-up activity for **The definition game (12)** from this section, or a pre-activity for **Word hopscotch (41)** from the Vocabulary within Written Discourse section.

Teacher's diary

How did the learners react to this activity? Make a note of any unusual reasons which your students gave. Would you change any of the procedures for next time?

Sample teaching material

Word cards:

surgeon	mechanic	artist	journalist
musician	gardener	cook	hairdresser
sportsman	tailor	model	photographer
postman	salesman		

Picture cards:

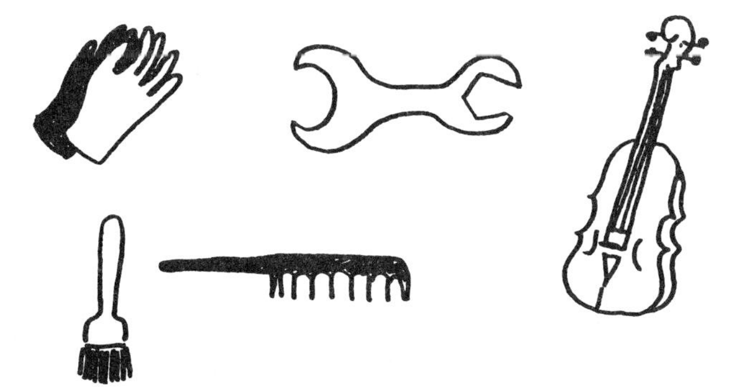

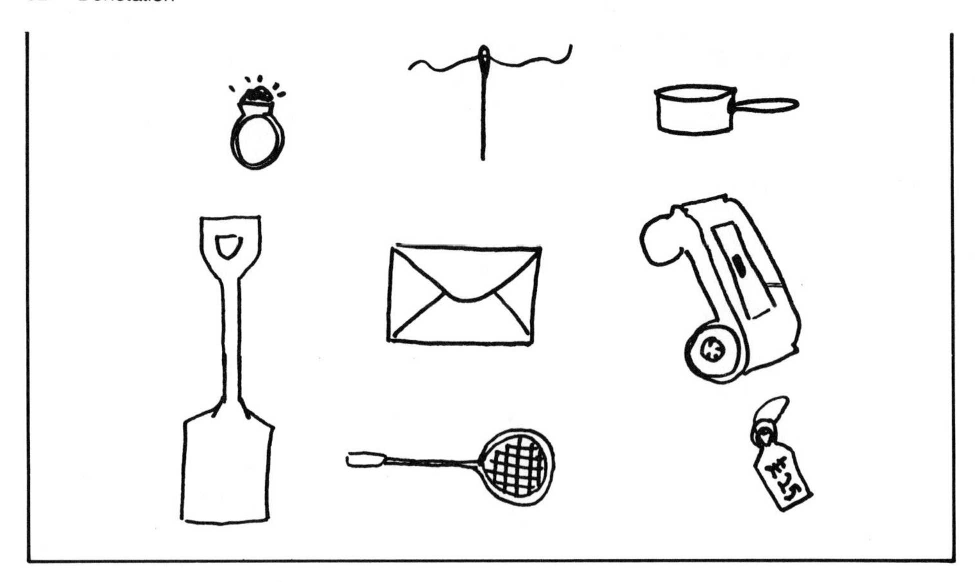

14 Instant recognition

Level	Elementary to intermediate
Students	All ages
Groups	Groups
Purpose	To familiarise learners with the meanings of common social sight phrases
Text type	Teacher's social sight phrases and matching exercise

In this activity

Learners discuss what is meant by common social sight phrases and where they might be encountered.

Preparation

Make flashcards for the social sight phrases given in the sample material for this activity, and copies of the related matching exercise. Alternatively, devise your own similar material.

In class

1. Divide your class into groups and give each group one social sight card, which they must not show to the other groups. Each group has to say (a) where a notice bearing their phrase might be found and (b) what the notice would mean.
2. Each group in turn gives the information required to the other groups, who try to guess what the notice says.
3. Give the correct meanings and contexts for the social sight phrases you have used, and then give out copies of your matching exercise. Groups work together to work out the answers, and, after an appropriate time, the whole class comes together to pool ideas and for feedback from you on the correct answers.

Link

With higher-level groups this activity could serve as a warm-up to **Misfits — the whole and the parts (39)** in the Register section.

Teacher's diary

How did the learners react to this activity? Were there any individual words which your learners misunderstood in these contexts? Would you change anything in the procedure for next time?

Sample teaching material

Social sight phrases for flashcards:

NOTHING TO DECLARE
VACANCIES
LOWER SALES FLOOR
KEEP CLEAR
NO THROUGH ROAD
AMUSEMENTS
UNDER TWOs ADMISSION FREE

Matching exercise:

Match each of the social sight phrases with its meaning (List A) and context (List B):

List A:

1. Small children can enter without charge.
2. There are still places left.
3. This is one storey where you can buy goods.
4. Do not park here.
5. Come this way if you have bought only permitted goods.
6. There is no way out.
7. This is a place where you can entertain yourself by playing arcade games.

List B:

1. In the window of a hotel.
2. On a garage door.

3. In the arrival lounge of an airport.
4. At the entrance to a cul de sac.
5. At the entrance to a shopping area.
6. At the entrance to a museum.
7. In a department store.

15 Hearing and visualising

Level Intermediate and above

Students Adults

Groups Whole class and pairs

Purpose To help learners understand abstract vocabulary through art and music, and through personal involvement

Text type Teacher's prepared story and related visual aids

In this activity

Learners share their personal responses to works of art or treasured possessions.

Preparation

This activity will need to span two sessions, because your learners will need to bring in objects from home for the second part. Choose a set of 'emotive words' for review, or use the sample material for this activity. Assemble objects of your own to illustrate what your learners will be required to bring, and relate them to relevant 'emotive words'. You could choose a painting, a cassette tape recording, or a treasured possession.

In class

1. Explain to your learners that art and music often inspire strong emotional responses. Show one of your chosen objects and ask for learners' reactions.

2. Show your set of 'emotive words' and see whether any of the reactions from Step 1 tally with words from that list. Invite learners to read the words on the list silently — do any well-known art works come to mind?

3. Show your remaining objects and ask for reactions before revealing your own feelings about each item. Explain your reasons for feeling as you do.

4. Set the task for the follow-up session: learners must bring from home a photo, picture, sculpture, cassette, etc. to illustrate one of the words from the 'emotive

words' list. This can be done as a free choice activity, or you can assign specific vocabulary items to specific learners.

5. Next session, have a 'show and tell' time in which learners share how they feel about what they have brought. This is less threatening if they tell each other in pairs first, without teacher intervention, and then report back to the whole class on what their partner said.

Link

This activity could serve as a warm-up to any from the Connotation section, such as **Positive/negative (36)**.

Teacher's diary

How did your learners react to this activity? Did they learn about each other through doing it? Would you change anything in the procedure for next time?

Sample teaching material

Emotive words:

ENIGMATIC	MACABRE	CLASSIC	INTRICATE
CHARMING	PERFECT	OFFENSIVE	TRIVIAL
UNCOUTH	SEMINAL	AWESOME	VIBRANT
EXCITING	SENSUAL	NOSTALGIC	DULL
SPINE-CHILLING	OLD-FASHIONED		

16 Experiencing is knowing

Level	Intermediate to advanced
Students	Adults
Groups	Whole class, then pairs or groups
Purpose	To convey the meaning of abstract vocabulary
Text type	Teacher's stories

In this activity

Learners build up a picture of what is meant by abstract words, through story telling, visual illustration and drama.

Preparation

Prepare your own list for review, or use the sample wordlist for this activity.

In class

1. Prepare stories to tell about words from the list, as in the sample teaching material for this activity. Tell the story for your first word.
2. Ask the learners how they would have felt in the situation you have described.
3. Tell learners the word you were in fact exemplifying and invite them to volunteer examples of their own of situations which have given rise to the same feeling in themselves.
4. Proceed to the next word, and so on.

Variation 1

Choose video clips instead of stories as examples.

Variation 2

Choose pictures to illustrate the words instead of stories.

Variation 3

The Handshake Game: Learners form two equal rows, facing each other. One partner shakes the other's hand in a way which corresponds to one of the words on the list. The partner must guess what the word is. The turn then passes to the other member of the pair, who must choose another word from the list to illustrate by a handshake, and so on.

Variation 4

'Mr Brown says he can't come.' This is a game for the whole class. Secretly show one learner a word from the list. The learners must then say the sentence about Mr Brown in such a way that the appropriate feeling will be conveyed. Whoever guesses the word correctly then takes the next turn, and so on.

Link

This activity could act as a lead-in, via **Overstating and understating (47)** in the Vocabulary in Spoken Discourse section, to work on intonation and attitude.

Teacher's diary

Which activity did you try? How did the learners react? Did the activity clear up ambiguities for the learners? Would you change the procedure in any way for next time?

Sample teaching material

List of 'feeling' words:

pleased	ecstatic	shocked	miserable
furious	disgusted	embarrassed	worried
afraid	smug	shy	confused

SECTION IV

WORD GRAMMAR

Introduction

There are five activities in this section:

17. Compound noun stress

18. Guess the stress

19. Suffix sorting

20. Add to it

21. The affix game

The activities in this section are concerned with breaking words down into component parts. They are also concerned with identifying a word's function from its form, e.g. whether it can act as noun, verb, adjective and so on. They include work on word stress, often linked to grammar, which can help learners to decode spoken English. The activities in this section therefore connect in three ways to work elsewhere in the book: on sound–spelling, polysemy and understanding spoken discourse. It is the relationship of pronunciation to word grammar which forms the basis of the first two activities in the section, while word classes and how they function are the focus of Activity 19. Both Activity 20 and Activity 21 explore the theme of affixation. The first two activities bring out the relationships between the form of a word, its sound and its meaning. The third activity links word form and word function, and the final two activities are wholly focused on word formation. All the activities in this section will help students to greater facility in using dictionaries, both in looking up the required word and in understanding the meaning of the coded entries.

17 Compound noun stress

Level Intermediate

Students All ages

Groups Whole class or groups

Purpose To sensitise learners to the effect of accurate stress placement on communication

Text type Teacher's list of compound nouns

In this activity

Learners practise varying stress so as to alter meaning.

Preparation

Make your own list of suitable compound nouns, or use the sample material for this activity.

In class

1. Distribute copies of your list of compound nouns. Model the first compound, first with stress on the first word and then with stress on the second. Ask your learners to describe the effect on meaning of the change in stress placement, and to think up sentences to illustrate their answer.

2. Have your learners work in groups to discuss the rest of the compound nouns in the same way. For lower levels, the whole wordlist can be dealt with as a whole class activity if preferred.

3. Bring the class together to hear the results of their discussions, and then give the key to the sample material, if used.

Link

I got rhythm (45) in the Vocabulary within Spoken Discourse section is another activity which explores how accurate stress placement helps to convey meaning.

Teacher's diary

How did the learners react to this activity? Were they able to imitate the shifting stress accurately? Would you change anything in the procedure for next time?

Sample teaching material

Compound noun list:

1. Quiet room	2. Black bird	3. Green house
4. Rain fall	5. Light blue	6. Foot rest

Key:

Stress on first word	Stress on second word
The quiet room is for private study	This is a nice, quiet room where we can talk
There's a blackbird on the lawn	Look at that big, black bird over there
I grow tomatoes in the greenhouse	My place is that little green house on the corner
The rainfall is expected to increase	Did the rain fall heavily?
He wore a light blue shirt with dark blue trousers	He wore a light, blue shirt over cotton trousers
Use the footrest if it's more comfortable	Let that foot rest a while because you've sprained it badly

18 Guess the stress

Level Intermediate to advanced

Students Adults

Groups Groups

Purpose To sensitise learners to some regularities in English word stress

Text type Teacher's wordlist

In this activity

Learners devise workable rules for English word stress.

Preparation

Use the sample teaching material for this activity, which has been chosen to exemplify the rules in the accompanying rule list. This activity is meant to reassure learners who are having difficulty making sense of word stress, so no exceptions have been included.

In class

1. Distribute copies of the wordlist and invite your learners to work in groups to mark where the main stress falls on each word. They should then try to devise rules for deciding where the stress should go, and be prepared to explain these rules to other groups.
2. Reshuffle the groups so that learners give their explanation to others.
3. Bring the whole class together to pool ideas, before you distribute the rule list for comparison.

Follow-up

Make a list of three- and four-syllable words having varied word stress and ask your learners to classify them according to stress pattern, e.g. 'mechanical' with 'particular' and 'telephonist', but 'teleprinter' with 'decorator' and 'interloper', etc. You can represent the categories visually with colours and shapes, e.g. ● • • • or with cuisinaire rods of different lengths.

Link

Both **Syllable snap (8)** from the Sound–Spelling section and **I got rhythm (45)** from the Vocabulary within Spoken Discourse section complement this activity.

Teacher's diary

How did the learners react to this activity? Did it appear to help their perception of word stress?

Sample teaching material

Words of three or more syllables:

millionaire	barbaric	employee	acoustics
mountaineer	insipid	coalesce	liquefy
picturesque	adoption	Vietnamese	astonish
connoisseur	altitude		

Words of two syllables:

conduct	convict	desert	incense	insult
present	rebel	record	reject	subject

Rule list:

Three-syllable words:

The endings which always carry main stress are:
-aire, -ee, -eer, -esce, -esque, -ese, -eur
The main stress always falls on the syllable immediately before these endings:
-ics, -id, -efy, -ion, -ish, -itude

Two-syllable words:

The stress falls on the first syllable when the word is acting as a noun, and on the second syllable when the word is acting as a verb.

19 Suffix sorting

Level	Intermediate to advanced
Students	Teenage to adult
Groups	Groups, whole class
Purpose	To help learners to see the connection between the form of a word and its function
Text type	Students' wordlists

In this activity

Students remember words with particular endings and categorise them according to function.

Preparation

None, but sample material is provided if appropriate. You may like your learners to work with dictionaries, depending on level.

In class

1. Divide learners into groups and ask them to work together to decide which of the following can be noun suffixes:
   -tion, -ment, -ness, -ic, -ful, -ive, -al, -ate.
2. Discuss as a whole class each group's findings.
3. Draw attention to the ambiguity of endings which are normally associated with adjectives (e.g. 'spoonful', 'directive') since they often become nouns in their own right. Mention clues from spoken English for words ending in -ate and -ment, which are pronounced differently when they are functioning as verbs from when they are functioning as nouns: in the former, the 'a' vowel is reduced to 'schwa' when the word is a noun, and in the latter, there is stress shift.

Link

Which sense (27) in the Polysemy section can be used as a follow-up activity to this one, since it also examines words which can be ambiguous in respect of word class and function.

Teacher's diary

How did the learners react to this activity? If you used the sample material, which endings caused most problems? Would you change anything in the procedure for next time?

Sample teaching material

-tion	*-ment*	*-ness*	*-ic*	*-ful*
creation	department	happiness	electric*	doubtful*
cremation	disarmament	witness**	frolic**	frightful*
degeneration	fragment**	harness**	harmonic**	cupful

-ive	*-al*	*-ate*
creative*	departmental*	demonstrate*
destructive*	detrimental*	graduate**
directive**	fractional*	precipitate**

Note:

* denotes that the word never functions as a noun

** denotes that the word *may* function as a noun

20 Add to it

Level Upper intermediate to advanced

Students All ages

Groups Whole class, divided into teams

Purpose To practise using common suffixes and prefixes

Text type Teacher's set of word roots

In this activity

Students play a team game in which they add beginnings and endings to common word roots.

Preparation

Prepare a set of flashcards from word roots on to which a prefix or a suffix can be added. Sample material is given for this activity. Have a dictionary handy to check the validity of student answers.

In class

1. Divide the class into teams — four is a number which allows team members to confer easily.
2. Hold up one of your flashcards, which should have plenty of white space around the root word depicted on it, so that learners can add to it.
3. Any team which can make another English word by adding to the beginning or ending wins a point. There is a bonus point for any team who can then add to the word further, e.g. MORAL — imMORAL — imMORALity. (Final 'e' can be deleted when a suffix is added, e.g. LOVing.)
4. Repeat the procedure with the other flashcards.
5. Add up team scores and declare a winner.

Link

This forms a warm-up activity for **The affix game (21)** from this section. It would also lead to **I got rhythm (45)** from the Vocabulary within Spoken Discourse section, and to **Making connections (29)** from the Polysemy section.

Teacher's diary

Which prefixes and suffixes were your students able to use most successfully? Would you change any of the game rules for next time?

Sample teaching material

List of word roots:

Proportion	Ration	Conserve	Harm	Real	Practice
Help	Depend	Comfort	Resist	Grace	Love
Establish					

21 The affix game

Level	Upper intermediate to advanced
Students	Teenage to adult
Groups	Groups
Purpose	To raise learner awareness of the meaning of some common suffixes
Text type	Teacher's affix cards

In this activity

Learners brainstorm examples of words with given affixes, and use them as the basis of a team game.

Preparation

Write some common affixes on separate pieces of card. You will need one card per group of students. You will also need dictionaries for students' use.

In class

1. Divide learners into groups and give each group, unseen by the others, one of your affix cards, e.g. dis-, -able, com-, re-, -or, -ment, etc.

2. Set a time limit — three minutes should be enough — for each group to make a list of six words bearing their affix, e.g. 'disagreeable', 'disfigure', 'disallow', 'discover', 'dispute', 'disappear'.

3. Set a further time limit — ten minutes should be ample — during which each group works with a dictionary to find an equivalent for each word on their list, e.g. 'disagreeable' = 'not very nice'. Monitor this activity and give help where needed.

4. Now begin the team game: one group reads out its words and phrases from Step 3. The other groups try to guess the affix concerned, winning a team point if successful. If nobody can guess, then the original group writes on the board its

wordlist from Step 2, minus the affix, i.e., for the examples given for Step 2, 'agreeable', 'figure', 'allow', 'cover', 'pute', 'appear'. Again, the other groups try to guess the affix and win a team point for doing so. The game continues until all groups have taken their turn. Scores are then added up and a winner declared.

Link

Sneaky spelling practice (9) from the Sound–Spelling section is another game concerned with form as well as content.

Teacher's diary

How did the learners react to this game? Did some affixes appear easier to work with than others? Would you change anything for next time?

SECTION V

COLLOCATION

Introduction

There are five activities in this section:

22. A bottle of beer

23. Pigeonholing words

24. Variations on a theme

25. Anticipation

26. Brainstorming prepositions

The activities in this section explore the connections between words — how words go together, either because of meaning similarities or because they stand beside each other in an accepted order combination. The section as a whole provides work on all points of the continuum from the wholly meaning-focused Activities 23 and 25, through a focus on both meaning and form (Activities 22 and 24) to the completely form-focused Activity 26. Activities 22 and 24 deal with difficulties in learning common fixed collocations by grouping them thematically. Activities 23 and 25 examine words which might be predicted within a given context. Activity 26 uses a brainstorming technique to reveal exactly which words can stand alongside common prepositions.

22 A bottle of beer

Level Elementary to intermediate

Students All ages

Groups Individual or groups

Text type Teacher's list of 'container' words, visual aids

In this activity

Students suggest suitable contents for different types of containers.

Preparation

Make your own worksheet, or use the sample material for this activity. Assemble realia to illustrate the different containers chosen.

In class

1. Show your learners several of the containers you have brought, and ask what might be found inside them. Correct the answers given where necessary.
2. Give out copies of your worksheet, and ask learners to complete it with the names of suitable contents. All learners should complete the first column, and fast finishers can try the second column.
3. As a whole class activity, discuss the answers which learners have given, and compare with the key.

Link

Working with gapped texts helps learners' comprehension and decoding of words in context. **Clozings (42)** from the Vocabulary within Written Discourse section would be an obvious follow-up activity to this one.

Teacher's diary

How did the learners react to this activity? Did they come up with any unusual collocations?

Sample teaching material

Below is a worksheet which has been completed by a native speaker:

Column 1:	Column 2:
1 a) a jar of jam	b) a jam jar
2 a) a pack of biscuits	b) a crisp packet
3 a) a tube of toothpaste	b) a toothpaste tube
4 a) a box of matches	b) a match box
5 a) a flask of coffee	b) a hip flask
6 a) a glass of wine	b) a wine glass
7 a) a sachet of sugar	b) a sauce sachet
8 a) a case of champagne	b) a suit case
9 a) a carton of milk	b) a milk carton
10 a) a can of coke	b) a coke can
11 a) a crate of beer	b) a milk crate
12 a) a bottle of beer	b) a milk bottle
13 a) a bowl of soup	b) a soup bowl
14 a) a cup of coffee	b) a coffee cup
15 a) a vase of flowers	b) a flower vase
16 a) a sack of potatoes	b) a ruck sack
17 a) a bag of sugar	b) a carrier bag
18 a) a drum of oil	b) an oil drum
19 a) a tin of paint	b) a paint tin
20 a) a pan of milk	b) a bed pan

23 Pigeonholing words

Level	Beginner to advanced, depending on input
Students	All ages
Groups	Groups
Purpose	Variation 1: to help learners develop the ability to categorise Variation 2: to acquaint learners with small differences in collocations, relating to sub-fields within a wider overall field
Text type	Teacher's word sets

In this activity

Learners classify words under headings of their own choosing, or make lexical sets by grouping words together under a given headword.

Variation 1

Preparation

Use the sample teaching material for this activity, or use your own similar word sets. The categories can be clear-cut for lower levels, or deliberately fuzzy for higher levels, as with the examples given here. Make word cards from your word sets so that learners can move words around in order to group and regroup them as they undertake the task of categorising.

In class

1. Divide the learners into groups and hand out the wordcards which you have prepared. Tell them that they must sort these wordcards into categories. Do not tell them what these categories should be, but ask them to provide titles of their own for each chosen category.

2. When all groups have had time to complete the task, bring the whole class together to hear their conclusions and their reasons for classifying the words as they did.

Variation 2

Preparation

Make copies of the wordlist for this activity, or devise your own.

In class

1. Write up on the board the following headings:
   THEATRE BALLET CONCERT EXHIBITION
   Distribute the wordlist to the learners, either as individuals, or to groups of three learners. Their task is to connect each word on the list with one of the headwords.
2. When everyone has had time to make a reasonable attempt at the task, bring the whole class together to pool ideas.

Link

Instant recognition (14) in the Denotation section explores connections of a different kind.

Teacher's diary

How did the learners react to this activity? Were there any unexpected categorisations?

Sample teaching material

Variation 1:

Wordlist for lower levels:

lamb	strawberry	lettuce	chicken
peach	carrot	beef	apple
onion	mutton	lemon	leek

Key:

MEATS: lamb beef mutton chicken
FRUITS: strawberry peach apple lemon
VEGETABLES: carrot lettuce onion leek

Wordlist for higher levels:

cycling cleaning floors jogging washing dishes
sewing stamp collecting making beds bird watching
walking in the mountains

Key:

SPORTS: cycling jogging walking in the mountains
HOBBIES: stamp collecting bird watching sewing

Note:

Some may think sewing is housework rather than a hobby. Others may think of walking as a hobby rather than a sport. Other category titles are possible, e.g. 'unpleasant duties', 'outdoor activities'

Variation 2:

Wordlist:

jazz	company	stage	solo	portrait
live	performance	comic	contemporary	photographic
classical	charity	lighting	production	score
design	one-man	pianist	choreographed	
masterpiece	script			

24 Variations on a theme

Level Elementary to advanced, depending on input

Students All ages, depending on input

Groups Groups, pairs, individuals

Purpose To aid learners' recall of idioms by grouping them according to theme

Text type Teacher's idioms, accompanying visuals and matching exercises

In this activity

Learners use known vocabulary to help them understand fixed collocations, relating to parts of the body, food, and sport.

Variation 1: Parts of the body — elementary

Preparation

Use the visuals and exercises given in the sample teaching material for this activity. Make an overhead transparency of the visuals if possible. Make copies of the matching exercise.

In class

1. As a whole class activity, revise common names for parts of the body by asking learners to list as many of them as they can remember within a time limit of one minute. Invite individuals to volunteer the ones they have named, and make sure that you have mentioned all the ones which will be needed in the matching exercise later.
2. Show the visuals and distribute the worksheet. Learners work in groups to match visuals with idioms and with meanings.
3. After an appropriate time, bring the whole class together to check answers.

Variation 2: Food — intermediate

Preparation

Using the food words given for this activity, assemble realia to illustrate them, or pictures for the same purpose. Make copies of the gap-filling exercise given in the sample material for this activity.

In class

1. Show the realia you have brought and invite learners to name the foods.
2. Divide the class into pairs or groups and distribute copies of the completion exercise. Learners must fill each gap with the name of one of the foods from the wordlist.
3. Bring the whole class together after a suitable time, to check answers and to explain the meaning of the idioms.

Variation 3: Leisure — advanced

Preparation

Use the sample material for this activity, i.e. the list of leisure activities and the list of idioms. Assemble visuals to illustrate the leisure activities listed, if possible.

In class

1. Show your chosen visuals, and ask learners to name the sports, games or hobbies depicted in them.
2. Invite learners to work in groups to brainstorm any idioms they might know which relate to sports, games and hobbies.
3. Give out copies of the leisure idioms and ask learners to work in pairs or groups to match each one to one of the leisure words and to decide on a plausible meaning for each.
4. Bring the whole class together after a suitable time, to check meanings. Discuss with learners possible situations in which each idiom might be used.

Link

Word-for-word translation (6) in the Mother Tongue Equivalence section is another activity based on fixed collocations.

Teacher's diary

Which theme did you choose? How did the learners respond to this activity? Would you change any of the idioms or anything in the procedure for next time?

Sample teaching material

Variation 1:

Match the visuals with an idiom and a meaning:

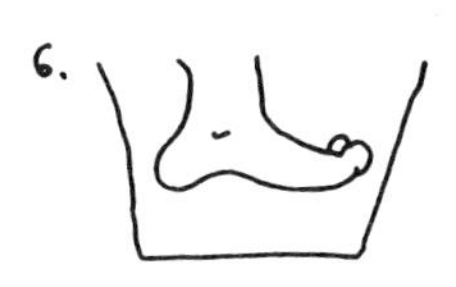

i) My heart bleeds for you
ii) I have eyes in the back of my head
iii) He hasn't a leg to stand on
iv) My ears are burning
v) He's two-faced
vi) I've put my foot in it

a) I know what your're doing — I can see everything
b) I've made a terrible mistake
c) Cheers!
d) Don't get angry
e) I can't do everything at once

vii) Bottoms up!
viii) I only have one pair of hands
ix) Keep your hair on!

f) He's not to be trusted
g) I think someone's talking about me
h) His argument is absolutely without foundation
i) I sympathise with you

Variation 2:

Complete the gap-filling exercise with a word from the wordlist:

Wordlist:

TEA APPLE BREAD CUCUMBER CAKE CHEESE
MILK BANANAS EGG BEANS PIE GOOSEBERRY

Gap-filling exercise:

1. She's the . . . . . of my eye. I love her.
2. He thinks he's the greatest thing since sliced . . . . .
3. You can't have your . . . . . and eat it.
4. There's no use in crying over spilt . . . . .
5. They're as different from each other as chalk and . . . . .
6. That boy is a real . . . . . head. He knows all the answers.
7. When I told him what had happened, he went . . . . .
8. That idea is just . . . . . in the sky. It will never happen.
9. Mary and John are going to the cinema tonight. If I go too, I'll be playing . . .
10. He's full of . . . . . tonight. He's just passed his driving test.
11. She was as cool as a . . . . . She didn't get nervous at all.
12. Basketball just isn't my cup of . . . . . I prefer football.

Variation 3:

Match each word from the list with an idiom. You may match more than one idiom to a single word:

Wordlist:

DIVING CRICKET PLAYGROUND GAMES CHESS
ATHLETICS CARD GAMES FOOTBALL HORSERIDING
TENNIS SKATING FISHING

Idioms:

1. I was bowled over by what happened.
2. I think he'll rise to the bait.
3. We're saddled with her mother again.

4. I'm for the high jump if I don't get it right.
5. Who will kick off?
6. I've got a few more cards up my sleeve.
7. What you lose on the swings you gain on the roundabouts.
8. He's diving in at the deep end with that one.
9. He's had a good innings.
10. I'm only a pawn in their game.
11. It's just not cricket!
12. Hold your horses!
13. The ball's in your court now.
14. Let's put all our cards on the table.

25 Anticipation

Level	Elementary to advanced
Students	All ages
Groups	Groups, pairs or individuals
Purpose	To activate students' background knowledge in order to help them predict likely vocabulary in a given text
Text type	Teacher's text

In this activity

Learners predict which vocabulary items will occur in a given text.

Preparation

Use a text which you are about to work on with the class. You will also need one large sheet of paper and several marker pens per group of learners. A visual appropriate to the theme of the text will also be useful. A sample text is given.

In class

1. Tell your learners that they are about to work with a text. Give them the title, show the accompanying visual if you have one, and give a few details which will help learners predict content. Tell learners the length of the text too. Invite them to predict up to twenty vocabulary items which they think will occur in the text: they must be 'content' words, not 'grammatical' words. For the sample text given in the material for this activity, you could say, 'I'm going to give you a reading passage about a girl's experiences at her new school. It's a mixed secondary school, and the text is called "The First Year". It's about 120 words long.'
2. Invite the learners to work in groups to write their predicted words — give out one sheet of paper and marker pens for each group.
3. When every group has at least ten words, ask them to display their lists for the

rest of the class to read. If possible, put them around the walls, so that they remain visible while you hand out copies of the text.

4. Invite your learners to read through the text quickly to see if any of the words they have listed do in fact appear.
5. Work on the text in your normal way.

Link

This activity forms a bridge to any of the activities in the Vocabulary within Written Discourse section.

Teacher's diary

How did your learners react to this activity? Make a note of how many words were predicted correctly so that each time you try the activity you can find out whether learners are improving in their ability to predict.

Sample teaching material

'Leila started attending her secondary school in September. After two to three weeks, the first-year children were assessed and graded. Leila's reading age was assessed as thirteen years, and her spelling age fifteen years. She was consequently allocated to a class in the top band, where she had none of her former classmates from primary school, and was therefore separated from her close friends. Leila was very outspoken and articulate and particularly enjoyed contributing to discussions. She found that she was the only girl to do so. I believe that many of the boys, particularly the dominant gorup, saw this as a threat to their control. The boys' response to behaviour they considered competitive was to attempt to intimidate Leila with racist and sexist abuse, threats and physical violence. Other girls avoided this attention by keeping quiet.'

26 Brainstorming prepositions

Level Upper intermediate to advanced

Students Adults

Groups Groups

Purpose To explore the many uses of these overworked English words

Text type Students' own word associations

In this activity

Learners brainstorm collocations for common prepositions.

Preparation

None. Bring to class a large piece of paper and several marker pens per group of learners. Dictionaries will also be useful for checking what learners produce.

In class

1. Tell your learners that you are going to give them a piece of paper on which you have written a very common English word — a preposition. Their task is to brainstorm words which (a) come before it, (b) come after it or (c) fit around it, e.g. 'up' could generate 'hold-up', 'upsurge' and 'go up the spout'. Sample brainstormings are given in the material for this activity.
2. Divide learners into groups and give them a piece of paper and markers on and with which to record their ideas. Depending on the size and level of the class, you can choose whether to set each group to work on the same word, or on different ones.
3. After an appropriate time, call the class together to share what they have produced, checking accuracy and meanings, and supplying further examples.
4. Post the results around the walls of the classroom, so that they can be used for

revision or consolidation. This activity is particularly suitable for revising phrasal verbs and idioms.

Link

Making connections (29) from the Polysemy section uses a similar brainstorming technique.

Teacher's diary

How did your learners react to this activity? Did they produce any incorrect collocations? Were these influenced by their mother tongue? Would you make any changes in the procedure for next time?

Sample teaching material

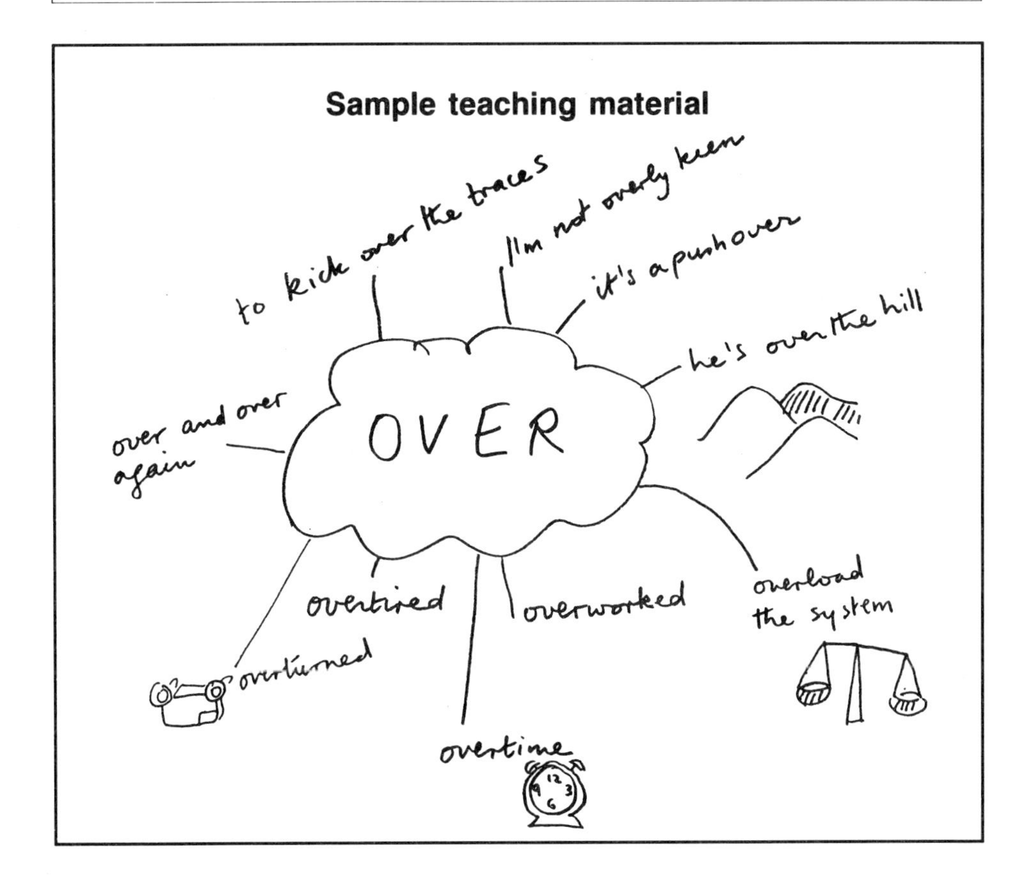

SECTION VI

POLYSEMY

Introduction

There are three activities in this section:

27. Which sense?

28. Double lives

29. Making connections

The activities in this section encourage learners to think about the possibility that a given word may have more than one meaning or more than one function. Often, learners assume that a word in context has the meaning and function which is most familiar to them. They are unaware that several interpretations exist, so that misunderstanding of the surrounding sentence, or even of the whole text, may result. If such a misunderstanding should arise with spoken discourse, then meaning cannot be recovered, and a breakdown in communication results. Activity 27 provides a useful warm-up exercise for work on any text. In it, learners provide synonyms for ambiguous words taken out of context and then substitute them for the originals in context. In Activities 28 and 29, learners work with items of vocabulary which have a frequent general meaning but also a more specific meaning within a particular field or discipline. These two activities will therefore be of especial relevance for learners of English for Specific Purposes, and they can be linked with activities from the Register section. Because of their emphasis on form, all of the activities in this section can be integrated with those in the Sound–Spelling section.

27 Which sense?

Level Intermediate to advanced, depending on input

Students Teenage to adult

Groups Individual, then group or whole class

Purpose To alert learners to the problems arising from words of ambiguous meaning or function

Text type Teacher's text

In this activity

Learners suggest synonyms for words taken out of context, then substitute them for the originals in context.

Preparation

Use the sample wordlist and text given as teaching material for this activity, or create your own.

In class

1. This step must be done by individual learners working alone: distribute the chosen wordlist and invite your learners to write against each word the first synonym — word or phrase — which comes to mind.
2. Now invite learners to share their answers with a partner or with several others, to see whether they have interpreted meanings differently.
3. Distribute copies of the text and invite learners to substitute their own synonyms for the original words. Ask several learners to read their versions aloud to the class. Do these make sense?

Link

This activity can be a warm-up to **Word hopscotch (41)** from the Vocabulary within Written Discourse section.

Teacher's diary

How did the learners react to this activity? Were they able to see alternative interpretations for all the words? Would you change anything in the procedure for next time?

Sample teaching material

Wordlist:

a) BRANCH .... b) TEAR ....
c) BILL .... d) INVALID ....
e) REFUSE .... f) DESERT ....

Text:

'Was that the phone? Not again!

'Mary went into the hall and picked up the receiver with shaking hand: "Hallo."

'"Good morning. Swann's, Retford BRANCH here. Is that Mrs Taylor?"

'"Oh. Yes."

'"I'm afraid the cheque you sent us in settlement of our BILL for £300 is INVALID. The bank REFUSE to pay it."

'"Oh, I'm terribly sorry. I'll contact them right away."

'"Thank you."

'She sank into a chair. Her usual confident manner had begun to DESERT her. A TEAR formed in the corner of her eye and slowly descended her ashen-white cheek . . .'

28 Double lives

Level	Intermediate to advanced, especially ESP learners
Students	Adults
Groups	Groups
Purpose	To introduce learners to some very frequent general English words which also have a second, quite specific, meaning
Text type	Teacher's word cards

In this activity

Learners find both a general and a specific meaning for given ambiguous words.

Preparation

Use the wordlist and list of specific fields given as sample material for this activity. Make word cards from the words on the list. Dictionaries for checking may be useful.

In class

1. Divide the class into groups of three or four learners. Deal six word cards to each group. Depending on level and time available, you can give all groups the same word set, or give each group a different set. Tell your learners that they must try to find a general meaning and another more specific meaning for the words on the cards. Advanced learners may be able to do this without help, but others may need the list of fields (given in the sample material) to help them.
2. Send one member of each group to another group, so that learners can pool answers.
3. Bring the whole class together for feedback. Were any of the meanings unfamiliar? Are any of the learners working in one of the specific fields given? Can any learners suggest other words with 'double lives'?

Note: The words given for this exercise have been chosen carefully so that they do not include words with ambiguous grammar as well as ambiguous meaning: all are nouns for the purposes of this exercise.

Link

Making connections (29) from this section is another activity which explores ambiguous words. **Misfits — the whole and the parts (39)** from the Register section makes a useful follow-up activity to this one.

Teacher's diary

How did the learners react to this activity? Make a note of the comments you made on Step 3. Would you change the procedure for next time?

Sample teaching material

Wordlist:

AIR	SERIES	MASS	POLE
PLATE	THEATRE	ENVELOPE	CELL
THREAD	TELLER	BALANCE	DIFFERENCE

List of specific fields:

MEDIA PURE SCIENCE MEDICINE COMPUTING
ELECTRICAL ENGINEERING MECHANICAL ENGINEERING
BANKING AND ACCOUNTS

Key:

Word	*Specific Field(s)*
Air	Media
Series	Media and Electrical Engineering
Mass	Pure Science
Pole	Pure Science
Plate	Mechanical Engineering and Medicine
Theatre	Media and Medicine
Envelope	Computing
Cell	Electrical Engineering and Medicine
Thread	Mechanical Engineering
Teller	Banking and Accounts
Balance	Banking and Accounts
Difference	Banking and Accounts

29 Making connections

Level	Upper intermediate to advanced, especially ESP learners
Students	Adults
Groups	Groups, whole class
Purpose	To prepare learners for the possibility of seeing a familiar word used in an unfamiliar way
Text type	Students' own words generated from teacher's wordlist

In this activity

Learners brainstorm examples of ambiguous words having general and specific meanings.

Preparation

Select a few of the words from the wordlist given in the teaching material for this activity. Write each in the centre of a separate piece of large paper — you will need one piece of paper between three to four learners. Make copies of the completion exercise given as teaching material for this activity, and of the key.

In class

1. Divide the class into groups and give each group some marker pens and a large piece of paper on which you have written one of the words from the list. Depending on level, you can give all the groups an identical word, or different ones.
2. Ask your learners to write or draw whatever comes to mind when they consider the word on the paper. Samples of such brainstormings are given in the teaching material for this activity.
3. Post the learners' efforts around the walls of the classroom and invite the learners to mill about looking at each other's ideas.
4. Gather the whole class together for feedback on what they have produced. Then distribute copies of the key and dictionaires.

5. Consolidate this work by giving out copies of the completion exercise for learners to work on, either in class or at home.

Link

Other activities which would be suitable for ESP learners are **Misfits — the whole and the parts (39)** from the Register section, and **Instructions — who for? (44)** from the Vocabulary within Written Discourse section.

Teacher's diary

How did the learners respond to this activity? Did the learners discover any specific meanings which you had not thought of? Would you change anything in the procedure for next time?

Sample teaching material

Wordlist:

AUTOMATIC	CHARGE	COUPLE	GUARD	MAIN	TENDER
PITCH	NET	BANK	CONTACT	TACK	KEY
SUPPORT	PRESS	PAGE			

Key:

Automatic — specific field: mechanics
Charge — specific field: military, electrical
Couple — specific field: mechanics
Guard — specific field: military
Main — specific field: utilities
Tender — specific field: business
Pitch — specific field: sport
Net — specific field: business
Bank — specific field: business
Contact — specific field: electrical
Tack — specific field: nautical
Key — specific field: music and computing
Support — specific field: engineering and medical
Press — specific field: media
Page — specific field: tourism

Completion exercise:

Fill the gaps with words from the wordlist:

1. There's a burst water . . . . ., so the traffic's been diverted.
2. The child has severe burns. What a shame the parents didn't have the fire . . . . . in place.
3. This steak isn't very . . . . . I think I'll send it back.
4. My salary is quite large when you look at the gross figure, but the . . . . . figure isn't very attractive at all.
5. I'm afraid I can't do that question. Let's cheat and look at the . . . . .
6. . . . . . Mr Smith, will you?
7. I'll just check to see whether we have that information in our data . . . . .
8. Well, as the spare part costs only £1.25 I don't think they'll make any . . . . .

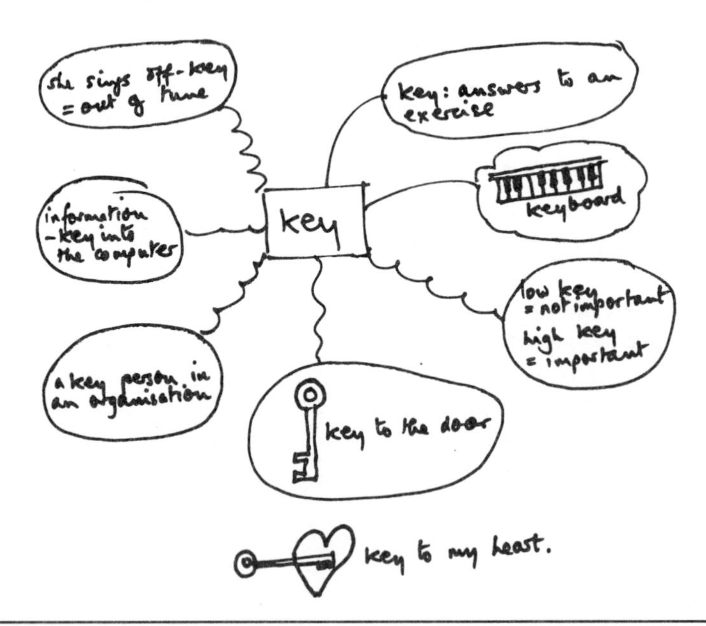

SECTION VII

FREQUENCY

Introduction

There are three activities in this section:

30. Vocabulary for recall

31. Playing the top ten

32. Brainstorming compounds

This section addresses the task of prioritising which vocabulary items to teach. Of course we would wish to teach those which are likely to be met most often. However, learners of English for Specific Purposes may need to know specialised vocabulary which is not frequently encountered in a general English context. Moreover, learners themselves may wish to learn infrequent items because of their personal interests or hobbies. The first activity in the section can be undertaken by students of any age, nationality or level, since it deals with the vocabulary items which they have remembered and why. Activity 31 is again appropriate to all types of learners and sensitises them to the very frequent occurrence of some English grammatical words. In Activity 32, learners try to make different two-word collocations and compare them with those which native speakers make most frequently. The activities in this section could be used as a lead-in to work on Collocation or Register.

30 Vocabulary for recall

Level Beginners to advanced, especially mixed-nationality groups

Students All ages

Groups Individual, groups or whole class

Purpose To explore reasons why words which are frequently used in English may not always be easy for learners to remember

Text type Learner-generated

In this activity

Learners test their own recall of English vocabulary and compare it with that of others.

Preparation

None. Copies of the frequency list given in the material for this activity may be useful.

In class

1. Ask your learners to work individually to write down, in two minutes, all the English words they can remember. These include 'grammatical words' like 'and' or 'that' as well as 'content words' like 'love' or 'summer'. Tell your learners that they should think especially of words which they suppose occur very frequently in English.
2. Ask your learners from groups to compare what they have written and to share reasons for remembering them, e.g. they may remember a whole scene evoked by a given word, which may not be at all evocative for other learners; they may remember an English word because it exists in their own language; they may remember an English word because it sounds like a word (perhaps a taboo word) in their own language; they may *not* remember a very frequent English word because it is very difficult for them to pronounce.
3. Follow up by distributing the frequency list for comparison.

Link

Marks on a paper (1) and **Sound feelings (4)** from the Mother Tongue Equivalence section could be used as preparation or follow-up.

Teacher's diary

How did the learners react to this activity? What did you discover about their own language(s)? Would you change anything in the procedure for next time?

Sample teaching material

The 200 most frequent items:

1	the	25	have	49	no	73	your
2	of	26	this	50	him	74	its
3	and	27	are	51	out	75	people
4	to	28	by	52	up	76	know
5	a	29	or	53	about	77	over
6	in	30	she	54	more	78	two
7	that	31	from	55	me	79	just
8	it	32	her	56	them	80	well
9	I	33	we	57	who	81	any
10	was	34	all	58	do	82	even
11	is	35	were	59	can	83	because
12	he	36	one	60	has	84	our
13	for	37	which	61	will	85	these
14	you	38	there	62	like	86	down
15	with	39	an	63	into	87	back
16	as	40	so	64	some	88	think
17	on	41	if	65	then	89	way
18	had	42	would	66	could	90	first
19	be	43	their	67	now	91	most
20	his	44	said	68	time	92	much
21	at	45	what	69	only	93	get
22	but	46	been	70	than	94	how
23	not	47	my	71	other	95	see
24	they	48	when	72	very	96	did

97	don't	123	come	149	same	175	quite
98	after	124	say	150	course	176	left
99	it's	125	got	151	great	177	every
100	man	126	being	152	men	178	place
101	where	127	going	153	always	179	under
102	go	128	work	154	I'm	180	small
103	new	129	right	155	want	181	find
104	too	130	long	156	children	182	used
105	may	131	off	157	though	183	looked
106	made	132	here	158	each	184	far
107	before	133	again	159	last	185	rather
108	should	134	take	160	three	186	fact
109	little	135	day	161	things	187	that's
110	us	136	old	162	why	188	nothing
111	many	137	yes	163	while	189	himself
112	good	138	might	164	both	190	women
113	through	139	world	165	really	191	around
114	such	140	life	166	Mr	192	enough
115	must	141	between	167	few	193	told
116	own	142	thought	168	look	194	since
117	still	143	came	169	didn't	195	part
118	also	144	another	170	without	196	end
119	never	145	something	171	against	197	home
120	years	146	went	172	thing	198	does
121	make	147	put	173	once	199	use
122	those	148	away	174	house	200	year

31 Playing the top ten

Level	Elementary to advanced
Students	All ages
Groups	Individual, pair, group, whole class
Purpose	To sensitise learners to the importance of 'little' English words which normally go unnoticed
Text type	Variation 1: Learner-generated text Variation 2: Teacher's gapped text

In this activity

Variation 1: Learners write texts which do not contain given words.
Variation 2: Learners use given words to reconstitute text.

The ten most frequent words in English — the top ten of the title — are: 'the', 'of', 'and', 'to', 'a', 'in', 'that', 'it', 'I' and 'was'. Here are two activities which explore this fact, and sample teaching material is given for both:

Variation 1:

Ask learners to write a sentence/paragraph/minisaga (a piece of writing using exactly fifty words) without using any/one/some of the given words.

Variation 2:

Delete some/all of the top ten words from a class text, and ask learners to try to replace the missing words. In particular 'it' and 'that' are capable of many functions and it may be instructive for learners to work with these two words.

Link

Clozings (42) in the Vocabulary within Written Discourse section is a natural follow-up to this activity.

Teacher's diary

How did the learners react to this activity? Which 'frequent words' in particular caused most problems?

Sample teaching material

Variation 1: A minisaga (fifty words exactly)

Boy travelling alone.
He's cold. He's hungry.
He hasn't eaten for three days . . .
Tired limbs. Tired head. Tired heart.
Look! . . . Lights over there! . . . Can he be dreaming?
Knock loudly . . . No answer.
Slowly . . . door opens.
My son!
My father!
After all these years. Journey's end.
Miracles happen.

Cloze text:

Which of the top ten words is represented by each number in the text below?

'(1) is noticeable (2) all (3) top ten words are short — (4) longest (5) them has only four letters. They are function words rather than content words: (6) is, they function more as (7) grammatical glue (8) holds our discourse together than (9) talk about facts, events (10) ideas (11) (12) world outside language. They fall into part-(13)-speech classes which have very few members. There are no representatives at all (14) (15) large part-(16)-speech classes (17) which most words belong — nouns, main verbs (18) adjectives.'

Key:

1. it	2. that	3. the	4. the	5. of	6. that
7. the	8. that	9. to	10. and	11. in	12. the
13. of	14. of	15. the	16. of	17. to	18. and

32 Brainstorming compounds

Level Intermediate to advanced, especially ESP learners

Students Adults

Groups Individual or groups, then whole class

Purpose To show how nouns can combine in English, and to encourage learners to experiment with different combinations

Text type Teacher's list of two-word nouns, visual aids

In this activity

Learners brainstorm the second word of English compound nouns.

Preparation

None. The sample material for this activity is a breakdown of the most frequent native speaker responses to the task given here. Copy the five words given in Step 1 below on to large paper, enough for one piece per group of learners.

In class

1. Tell your learners that you are going to give them a piece of paper on which you have written the first half of five compound nouns, namely:
   SCHOOL, WATER, FASHION, INDEX and TAX.
   Their task is to find another word which could follow each, thus forming a compound noun. Give a few examples to help the learners, e.g. LUNCH BOX, PENCIL CASE, LAMP POST.
2. Divide the learners into groups and give each group some markers and the paper. Allow time for them to complete the task.
3. Call the class together for feedback on what they have produced. Then distribute copies of the native speaker responses.

Follow-up

Alert learners to the role of stress in compound nouns: those which function as a single lexical item have the stress on the first syllable.

Link

Brainstorming prepositions (26) in the Collocation section uses a similar technique. **Variations on a theme (24)** from the same section would be a useful follow-up.

Teacher's diary

How did the learners react to this activity? How did the compounds which they suggested differ from the native speakers'?

Sample teaching material

The most frequent native speaker responses:

Word	First choice	Second choice	Third choice
SCHOOL	DINNER	DAYS	TEACHER
WATER	FALL	TAP	BOARD
FASHION	SHOW	PARADE	HOUSE
INDEX	FINGER	FILE	CARD
TAX	CODE	BILL	EVASION

Other native speaker responses:

SCHOOL holidays/bus
FASHION magazine/model/show
WATER tank/jug/bed
TAX return/inspector

SECTION VIII

CONNOTATION

Introduction

There are four activities in this section:

33. Kelly's eye view

34. Sounding out

35. Advertising adjectives

36. Positive/negative

Once learners have reached an intermediate level of competence in English, they run the risk of using a word inappropriately, either because it is taboo, derogatory or over-familiar. This section provides activities which explore hidden meaning. Learners themselves may have a liking for, or an aversion to, particular words in English, which they can discover by working through the classification procedure in Activity 33. Activity 34 deals with common English words for sounds. Activity 35 explores students' reactions to common English adjectives used in advertising. Activity 36 gives a technique for exploring connotation which can be used with any random vocabulary list. Since all these activities involve the students in group work on problem solving, analysis and introspection, they are more appropriate for adults and work most successfully, though not exclusively, with multilingual groups.

33 Kelly's eye view

Level Elementary to advanced, depending on input

Students Teenage to adult

Groups Groups, then whole class

Purpose To review vocabulary

Text type Vocabulary list for review

In this activity

Learners compare and contrast items of vocabulary according to their own criteria.

This is an application of Kelly's Repertory Grid technique which is designed to fix in memory vocabulary already met.

Preparation

Use the teaching material from this activity, or make your own list of about fifteen words for review. Transcribe each word on to a piece of card — this makes one card set. Duplicate this card set so that you have one set per group of learners. If possible make the vocabulary list from words the students themselves have chosen to record, rather than the words you have 'taught.'

In class

Demonstrate the first four steps of the procedure with one group first, before giving out card sets to other groups:

1. Appoint a group secretary for each group and give her/him a sheet of paper and a pen.
2. The secretary shuffles the pack of cards and places it face-down in the centre of the table.
3. The secretary turns up three cards and places them alongside each other. The first player must group them as two and one: two cards which are similar in some

way, and one which is somehow different. S/he must also give reasons for her/his choice. For the sample material given, one student linked 'prohibit' with 'stand up' because he saw them as commanding him to do something, but 'transplant' was different.

4. The secretary records the classification and reasons given under three headings, 'Same', 'Different', 'Reasons', thus:

Same	*Different*	*Reasons*
'prohibit' 'stand up'	'transplant'	Both command me to do something

The turn passes to the next player, who classifies the next three words in the same way, and so on until all words are used up.

5. When all groups have finished, bring the class together for discussion and feedback on the classifications made and why.

Variation

The above procedure has been applied to an unstructured vocabulary list, but you could use vocabulary linked thematically, e.g. parts of the body — 'eyes', 'teeth', 'head' — 'eyes' and 'teeth' are similar because they are parts of a whole, but 'head' is not.

Link

This is a content-focused method of reviewing vocabularly. **Spelling puzzles (7)** from the Sound–Spelling section is a form-focused equivalent.

Teacher's diary

How did the learners react to this activity? Did any of the classifications surprise you? Which?

Sample teaching material

One learner's vocabulary list made over a four-hour teaching day. The words he chose to learn were:

PROHIBIT
CABBAGE
ARTICLE
VIOLENT
ANNIVERSARY
MEMORY
SWEEP
TRANSPLANT
STROKE
AFFAIR
INVITATION
ORGANISE
POLITE
HELMET
STAND UP
MOVE
FAITHFUL
NATURALLY
CUPBOARD
FESTIVAL
BRUSH
KICK
HANDSOME
OVERDRAFT
STAGE
COST

34 Sounding out

Level Intermediate to advanced

Students Teenage to adult

Groups Whole class and groups

Purpose To explore the connotations of some common 'sound words' in English

Text type Teacher's sound set, worksheet, audio aids

In this activity

Learners listen to sounds, then discuss names for the sounds and possible contexts for use.

Preparation

The activity is based on English names for sounds. You will need to choose which ones to present, then prepare either (a) to demonstrate the sounds yourself in class, (b) to make a recording of the sounds for use in class or (c) to use a commercially produced sound recording (see Reference section). You will also need a related worksheet. A sample 'sound word' list and accompanying worksheet is given in the material for this activity.

In class

1. Introduce the activity by demonstrating two or three sounds and inviting learners to say (a) how they would describe the sound and (b) what would normally make the sound, e.g.:

   CLICK:
   (a) short, repeated, soft, not polite if used to attract attention . . .
   (b) made by human fingers, or by container as it is closed . . .

2. Present everyone with a copy of your complete 'sound word' list, and ask learners to work in groups to describe each sound, as they did in Step 1.

3. Bring the class together to hear the sounds on the wordlist and to check answers.
4. Distribute copies of the worksheet, and ask learners to complete the sentences.

Follow-up

1. Use your sounds as the basis for a writing exercise in which learners make a narrative which includes them all.
2. Examine the effect of using a word with 'animate' connotations to describe what is normally regarded as 'inanimate', e.g.: 'The powerful engine *growled* and *grunted* impatiently at slow speeds, but at sixty miles an hour the *growling* stopped and the motor began to *purr* with pleasure.'

Link

This could lead into or follow **Sound feelings (4)** from the Mother Tongue Equivalence section, or provide a warm-up activity for **Positive/negative (36)** in this Connotation section.

Teacher's diary

How did the learners react to this activity? Did you find out anything new about 'sound word' connotations in your learners' mother tongue(s)?

Sample teaching material

List of 'sound words':

SCREECH	WHISPER	SCRATCH	SIGH	BARK
TAP	PURR	WHISTLE	GRUNT	HUM
SHOUT	GROWL	RATTLE	SNORT	

Completion exercise:

Complete each sentence in a suitable way:

1. The housewife slammed .....
2. The manager tapped .....
3. There was a scratching .....
4. In the distance, we heard the hum .....
5. She let out a sigh .....

Key (One native speaker's response):

1. The housewife slammed the door in the salesman's face.
2. The manager tapped his pencil on the desk, to call the meeting to order.
3. There was a scratching at the door, but it was only the cat wanting to come in.
4. In the distance, we heard the hum of motorway traffic.
5. She let out a sigh of relief when the judge pronounced her 'not guilty'.

35 Advertising adjectives

Level Intermediate to advanced

Students Teenage to adult

Groups Whole class, individual, or group

Purpose To show the positive bias of some English adjectives which are popular in the field of advertising

Text type Teacher's authentic advertisements, list of adjectives and list of products for advertising

In this activity

Learners complete a grid by choosing the most appropriate adjectives to use for advertising various products, and compare their choice with authentic advertisements.

Preparation

The sample material for this activity gives a list of products, a list of adjectives, a grid and authentic advertisements. Make enough copies of the blank grid and of the wordlist so that each learner has one of each.

In class

1. Write on the board the list of products. Choose one product from the list and invite learners to say how they would attract people to buy it.
2. Distribute copies of the list of adjectives, which is taken from the authentic advertisements used as sample teaching material for this activity, and elicit from your learners which of them would be appropriate for the product you chose in Step 1.
3. Distribute copies of the blank grid, and invite your learners to work in groups to predict which adjectives fit which products, ticking the appropriate boxes.
4. Reveal the completed grid, as given in the sample material, which shows how the words from the adjective list are distributed in the authentic English

advertisements. This can be done most effectively using the overhead projector, so that you can reveal each line at a time. Discuss how the grid might differ from learners' grids, and which adjectives seem to be in vogue for advertising in your learners' mother tongue(s), as well as in English.

Follow-up

1. Present some authentic advertisements, English or not, for comparison. Sample advertisements are given in the teaching material for this activity.
2. Invite your learners to write their own advertisements for one of the products from Step 1.

Link

Misfits — the whole and the parts (39) from the Register section is another activity which develops learners' ability to match vocabulary items appropriately to text type.

Teacher's diary

How did your learners react to this activity? What did you learn about 'advertising vocabulary' in your learners' mother tongue(s)?

Sample teaching material

List of products:

catalogue of electrical goods
dictionary
hotel
tin of paint
gas boiler
baby carriage
new type of textile
credit card

List of adjectives:

ACCURATE	BEAUTIFUL	BEST	BRIGHT	CLEAN
COMFORTABLE	COMPREHENSIVE	EASY	EXCEPTIONAL	FAMOUS
FINE	EXCITING	FREE	FULL	NEW
GUARANTEED	HARD-WEARING	HEALTHY	IDEAL	SIMPLE

IMPROVED PEACEFUL UP-TO-DATE
INTIMATE SPECIAL USEFUL
INVALUABLE SUPERIOR
LEADING THOROUGH
SMOOTH UNIQUE

	catalogue	dictionary	hotel	paint	boiler	buggy	cloth	cr. card
accurate	√							
beautiful			√	√				
best	√	√	√					
brighter	√							
cleaner					√			
comfortable			√					
comprehensive		√						
easy/ier	√	√		√		√		
exceptional			√					
exciting				√				
famous	√							
fine							√	
free					√			√
full	√	√						
guaranteed			√					
hard-wearing				√				
healthier					√			
ideal			√	√				
improved		√						
intimate			√					
invaluable		√						
leading							√	√
new		√		√	√			√
peaceful			√					
simple	√	√						
smooth				√				
special					√			
superior				√			√	
thorough		√						
unique				√			√	√
up-to-date		√						
useful						√		

The GORE-TEX® fabric label says a lot about a garment.

It says that it's made from the world's finest performance fabric.

A fabric which outperforms all other outdoor fabrics comfortably.

Proof against wind, rain and snow. Yet breathable, so perspiration isn't trapped inside.

Found only in leading garments of superior construction, GORE-TEX fabric is the choice of experienced backpackers, ramblers and climbers.

So if you enjoy the outdoor life too, insist on the GORE-TEX fabric label.

DULUX ONCE

An exciting new product, for people who care about their home, Dulux Once has been specially developed by ICI to give a unique combination of convenience and performance-superior coverage in one coat.

Once Gloss is easy to use, being drip-resistant and self-undercoating. For use inside and out, it gives a beautiful gloss finish that is tough and hardwearing.

Once Emulsion is ideal for interior walls and ceilings, providing an attractive smooth silk finish. Made with ICI vinyl, it is tough, hardwearing and easily wiped clean.

The Marlborough

LONDON
A CREST EXCLUSIVE HOTEL

A beautiful Edwardian style hotel that offers comfort and service normally associated with a bygone age. Luxury is the order of the day; all 169 bedrooms are of Executive standard with in-house movies and there's a choice of Suites available for that extra special occasion. The Brasserie Bar with its resident pianist is a peaceful rendezvous before sampling the fine French Cuisine in the Brasserie Saint Martin. The hotel provides a valet service to the nearby NCP car park. All in all, an exceptional four star hotel with an intimate atmosphere of its own for those who appreciate the better things in life.

Luxury Theatre Breaks ... A speciality of the Marlborough. For guaranteed best shows and best seats call the hotel direct.

Around and about ... An ideal situation. Just across the road from the British Museum, with Covent Garden, Theatreland, Oxford Street, Regent Street and Tottenham Court Road tube just a short walk away.

The Marlborough, London
Enjoy a complimentary glass of champagne or Bucks Fizz with Sunday morning breakfast at The Marlborough Christmas programme.

36 Positive/negative

Level	Intermediate to advanced
Students	Adults
Groups	Whole class, groups
Purpose	To sensitise learners to some connotations of common words
Text type	Teacher's wordlist, survey grid

In this activity

Students discuss their perceptions of the connotations of some given English words.

Preparation

Make copies of the grid given in the sample material for this activity. The sample wordlist is a random one taken from the 'p' section of the *Longman Dictionary of Contemporary English*. Alternatively, make your own wordlist, either randomly from a dictionary, or from vocabulary items which you have recently taught to your class.

In class

1. Take one of the words from your list, and find out how your learners perceive its connotations in terms of the parameters 'Masculine/Feminine', 'Positive/ Negative', 'Animate/Inanimate'; e.g. the word 'petty' seems to be perceived by native English speakers to be rather negative, inanimate in fixed expressions such as 'petty cash' but otherwise used of humans, and more likely than not to be applied to females.
2. Give out copies of the empty grid, and invite learners to work in groups to discuss the connotations of the words on the left-hand side, ticking appropriate boxes.
3. Bring the class together to pool their responses, and to compare these with the native speaker ones given in the completed grid in the sample material for this activity.

Link

A useful warm-up activity for this one is **What did you call me? (3)** from the Mother Tongue Equivalence section, which also exploits connotations of single words.

Teacher's diary

How did the learners react to this activity? Did they often have conflicting views about a given word?

Sample teaching material

Wordlist:

PETTY PHYSIQUE PICTURESQUE PIERCING
PIG-HEADED PLUCKY

Completed grid (compiled from native speaker sample responses):

	Negative	Positive	Animate	Inanimate	Masculine	Feminine
PETTY	√		√	√	(√)	√
PHYSIQUE		√	√		√	
PICTURESQUE		√		√		(√)
PIERCING	√		√	√		
PIG-HEADED	√		√		√	(√)
PLUCKY		√	√			√

SECTION IX

REGISTER

Introduction

There are four activities in this section:

37. Photofits

38. Say it with feeling

39. Misfits — the whole and the parts

40. Transposition

This section is concerned with acquainting learners with the appropriateness of vocabulary: the easiest way to explore the concept of register is contrastively, e.g. informal versus formal, friendly versus belligerent, where context of situation can be taken into account. The first activity explores differences between written and spoken English, and Activity 38 examines further the formal/informal parameter. Activity 39 leads learners into an examination of whether certain vocabulary items are pertinent to certain text types. Activity 40 gives learners the opportunity to present the same information within different text types. While Activity 37 is suitable for all ages and levels, and Activity 40 could be tried by teenagers of intermediate level, most of the activities require some analysis of the language and understanding of the intentions of speakers and writers. They are therefore more appropriate for older and more advanced learners. Work from this section links well to activities from the Polysemy and Vocabulary within Discourse sections.

37 Photofits

Level	Elementary to advanced
Students	All ages
Groups	Groups
Purpose	To sensitise learners to some of the differences between spoken (informal) and written (formal) language in the reporting of past events
Text type	Student-generated, from visuals

In this activity

Learners use photos as the basis for a narrative or for work on direct speech.

Preparation

Assemble a set of photographs which can be used to tell a story. A class outing would be ideal. Sample photos are given as material for this activity.

In class

1. Divide the class into groups and distribute copies of the chosen photos. Post the originals on a large piece of paper on the class wall, with a title, and with ample space beneath each photo for a commentary. Ask your learners to work in their groups to devise a narrative for the pictures. They can work on the whole photo set, or on individual photos, depending on level and time available.
2. When the groups have finished, discuss what they have written and decide together on the narrative which best fits each photo. Invite the learners to write up the chosen narrative in the spaces beneath the original photos.

Variations

1. Instead of photos, cartoon strips can be used as the basis for student-generated narrative.

2. Instead of a photo set, single photos from newspapers can be used, their accompanying report read, and speech bubbles created, using the information from the report.
3. The suggested photos can be used, but instead of making a narrative, learners write bubbles for the photos to create a spoken commentary. This procedure is more appropriate for advanced learners, since the visual information has to be interpreted: the writer must take on the role of the person(s) in the photo(s).

Link

This activity works well with visual learners, and other such activities include **Marks on a paper (1)** from the Mother Tongue Equivalence section, and **Colour-coded sounds (10)** in the Sound–Spelling section.

Teacher's diary

How did the learners react to this activity? Which version did they prefer and why?

Sample teaching material

Written captions:

1. We sat on a log but it was not high enough.
2. So we were going to climb a tree, but it was difficult.

'Get off! This is my log.'

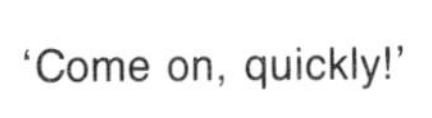

'Come on, quickly!'

38 Say it with feeling

Level Intermediate and above

Students Adults

Groups Groups, pairs, whole class

Purpose To raise awareness of the relationship between formal/impersonal and informal/personal spoken language

Text type Teacher's jumbled list of utterances

In this activity

Learners discuss possible contexts for given pairs of utterances and construct dialogues of formal, neutral and informal language.

Preparation

Make copies of the jumbled list given as sample material for this activity, or use your own similar phrases of spoken English.

In class

1. Distribute copies of the jumbled list of phrases and invite your learners to make pairs of utterances with similar meaning. Each pair will consist of one formal/impersonal phrase matched with an informal/personal one. Learners can do this in groups, pairs or individually. Check with the key afterwards.
2. Invite your learners to rank the phrases according to the amount of emotion expressed. Ask a few learners to read aloud the one they thought had the most emotion. Did that emotion come across to their audience?
3. Working with the whole class, ask your learners to volunteer a context for one or two of the utterances — who could have said it? To whom? In what situation? Sample suggestions are given in the teaching material for this activity.
4. Discuss with the whole class which utterances are formal and which informal. Are there some from which it is impossible to tell how the speaker feels?

5. Divide the learners into pairs and assign to each pair one of the given utterances. Ask them to work together to construct a short dialogue based on their phrase. Samples are given in the material for this activity.

Link

Overstating and understating (47) in the Vocabulary within Spoken Discourse section would be a relevant follow-up activity to this one.

Teacher's diary

How did the learners react to this activity? Did they find the informal phrases more difficult to deal with than the formal?

Sample teaching material

Jumbled list of phrases:

1. He passed away last Tuesday.
2. Put a sock in it.
3. What the hell are you doing here?
4. I should get a bigger one if I were you.
5. It was absolutely bucketing down.
6. Don't move!
7. I advise you to try the next size up.
8. You are requested to remain seated.
9. There has been torrential rain.
10. Could I ask you to make a little less noise?
11. He kicked the bucket on Tuesday.
12. Fancy meeting you here after all this time!

Key:

Formal		*Informal*
1	with	11
10	with	2
12	with	3
7	with	4
9	with	5
8	with	6

Suggested contexts:

10. Landlady to lodger who has been staying with her for only a few days. The lodger is playing loud music at night:

    LANDLADY: *Could I ask you to make a little less noise?* I really need to sleep now. I have to get up early in the morning for work.

    LODGER: Oh, I'm terribly sorry, I didn't realise the time! I've been working on this essay for tomorrow's lesson. I'll turn off the music straight away.

    LANDLADY: Thanks. I'll see you in the morning. Good night.

2. One student to another in the neighbouring room. One wants to study and his neighbour's loud music is distracting him:

    A: *Put a sock in it*, will you? I'm trying to work.

    B: Oh sorry, Jim. I've just bought this new album and its really good. I'll turn it down.

    C: Ta, mate. See you.

8. Air hostess to passengers beginning their flight:

    AIR HOSTESS: *You are requested to remain seated* and to refrain from smoking whenever the red light is showing . . .

6. Bank robber to bank employees:

    BANK ROBBER: *Don't move!* Keep your heads down, and you won't get hurt.

    EMPLOYEE: Aaagh!

    BANK ROBBER: I said don't move! . . . Now where's the safe?

39 Misfits — the whole and the parts

Level	Upper intermediate to advanced, especially ESP learners
Students	Adults
Groups	Groups or individuals, then whole class
Purpose	To give learners an appreciation of 'genre',* and of the fact that vocabulary alone does not make discourse recognisable as belonging to one particular genre rather than another
Text type	Teacher's authentic texts

In this activity

Learners predict vocabulary according to text type, match wordlists to given genres, and produce examples of writing appropriate to given genres.

Preparation

The sample teaching material for this activity includes a selection of genre extracts — a poem, a horoscope, an informal letter, a recipe, a sports report and a weather forecast — and a list of words from these extracts which would be appropriate for other genres as well as the original. Make enough copies of the wordlist for one copy per group of learners, and make enough copies for everyone of the authentic extracts.

In class

1. Ask your learners, working in groups, to write down five or six words which they might expect to find in a poem, a horoscope, an informal letter, a recipe, a sports report or a weather forecast. Depending on level, each group can do

* 'Genre', as defined by John Swales, is: 'A more or less standardised communicative event with a goal or set of goals mutually understood by the participants in that event and occurring within a functional rather than a social or personal setting' (full reference given on p. 190).

the task for all these genres, or you can assign a different genre to each group of learners.

2. After an appropriate time, bring the class together to hear the vocabulary generated by the task.
3. Distribute copies of the wordlist given as sample teaching material, and ask your learners to match each word set to a corresponding genre, chosen from POEM, HOROSCOPE, INFORMAL LETTER, RECIPE, SPORTS REPORT or WEATHER FORECAST. This task can be done in the same groups as before. Note that there are five wordlists but six genres: this makes for more discussion.
4. After an appropriate time, bring the class together again to discuss what they have decided and why, before distributing the authentic extracts for comparison.

Follow-up

Invite your learners to use one of the word sets from Step 3 of this activity to produce a piece of writing in *another* genre; e.g., if they thought the HOROSCOPE list was from a POEM, ask them to use it to *write a poem*. Check learners' efforts and display for all to read.

Link

Double lives (28) and **Making connections (29)** from the Polysemy section would complement this activity, particularly for learners of English for Specific Purposes.

Teacher's diary

How did your learners react to this activity? Did it throw up stereotypes in the vocabulary suggested?

Sample teaching material

Wordlist:

Word set 1: romance, dawning, time, commitment, trust
Word set 2: success, enjoy, joining, love, welcome
Word set 3: shared, within, inspired, wind-assisted, adversity
Word set 4: melt, centre, heat, low, continue, gently
Word set 5: smooth, wind, delicate, straight, dust

Key:

Word set 1: Horoscope, Word set 2: Letter, Word set 3: Sports report, Word set 4: Recipe, Word set 5: Poem

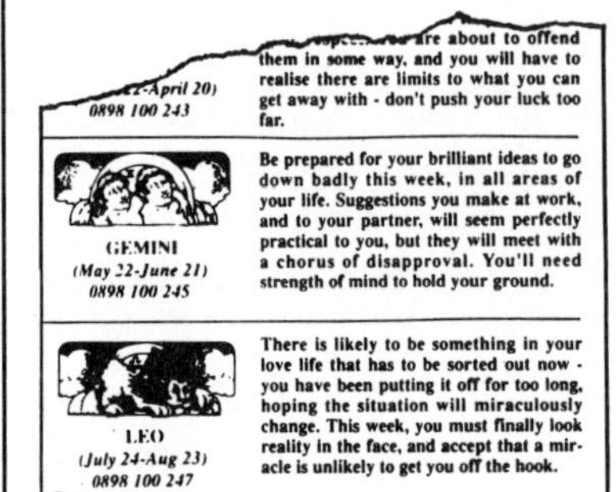

...are about to offend them in some way, and you will have to realise there are limits to what you can get away with - don't push your luck too far.

...-April 20)
0898 100 243

GEMINI
(May 22-June 21)
0898 100 245

Be prepared for your brilliant ideas to go down badly this week, in all areas of your life. Suggestions you make at work, and to your partner, will seem perfectly practical to you, but they will meet with a chorus of disapproval. You'll need strength of mind to hold your ground.

LEO
(July 24-Aug 23)
0898 100 247

There is likely to be something in your love life that has to be sorted out now - you have been putting it off for too long, hoping the situation will miraculously change. This week, you must finally look reality in the face, and accept that a miracle is unlikely to get you off the hook.

...the broth, and

Source: *The Retford Times*, 15 February 1990

15, Beverley Road.
23rd January.

Dear Linda, Tom and all,

Thanks so much for the money you sent for the girls for Christmas. It was a great success. They enjoy extending their Christmas by spending money afterwards. Soon your little one will be joining them I expect.

We should love to see you if you are down our way in the Summer. We shall be going away on 27th July for about 2 weeks, but you'd be very welcome at any other time.

Love to all,
Sandie.

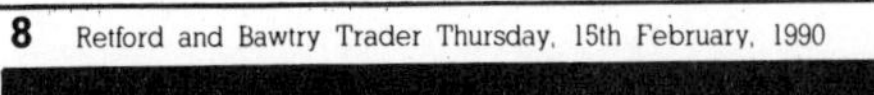

8 Retford and Bawtry Trader Thursday, 15th February, 1990

TRADER SPORT

All square at Bawtry

BAWTRY '88 Reserves shared six goals in their home game with Frames, despite leading by two goals at one stage.

An early lead went to Frames within the first ten minutes but Bawtry went into the interval on level terms thanks to an equaliser from skipper Dave Coates. After the break Bawtry came out inspired and straight from the kick off took the lead through a long wind-assisted shot from Hugh Harvey. A second goal from Coates took them into a 3-1 lead which looked to be decisive when Frames had a player dismissed for arguing with the referee.

But the visitors responded to this adversity and fought their way back into the game thanks to a gallant effort from the ten men. In the last fifteen minutes of the game they notched a couple of goals for a final score of Bawtry '88 Reserves 3, Frames 3.

EVERTON showed their ... probable first performers next by pulling back ... goal down to ... hard and ...

Source: *Retford and Bawtry Trader*, 15 February 1990

DECEMBER

Christmas Eve Dinner

Lobster Newburg

PREPARATION TIME: *15 min.*
COOKING TIME: *30 min.*

INGREDIENTS:

2 large cooked lobsters
6 oz. unsalted butter
6 large slices white bread
5 fluid oz. sherry or Madeira
1 tablespoon brandy (optional)
Salt and black pepper
3 egg yolks
$\frac{1}{2}$ pint double cream
Paprika

Carefully extract the meat from the tails and claws of the lobsters* and cut it into $1\frac{1}{2}$–2 in. pieces. Trim six circles from the bread and leave to soak in 4 oz. melted butter until this has been absorbed. Bake the butter-soaked bread on a baking tray in the centre of the oven for 25 minutes, at 300°F (mark 2).

Meanwhile, melt the remaining butter in a heavy-based pan, add the lobster meat and season with salt and pepper. Heat through over very low heat for 5 minutes, then pour over the sherry or Madeira and brandy. Continue cooking over very low heat until the wine has reduced* by half, after 10 minutes. While the lobster is cooking, beat the egg yolks and stir in the cream.

Remove the pan from the heat and pour the egg and cream mixture over the lobster. Shake the pan until the cream has mixed thoroughly with the wine, then move it gently to and fro over gentle heat until the sauce has the consistency of thick cream. Do not stir, or the meat will disintegrate and the sauce curdle. After about 3 minutes the lobster should be ready. Adjust seasoning and spoon the lobster and sauce on the bread rounds. Sprinkle the lobster with a little paprika and serve at once.

Boeuf Bourguignonne

PREPARATION TIME: *30 min.*
COOKING TIME: *3 hours*

INGREDIENTS:

2 lb. top rump of beef, cut into 2 in. cubes
4 oz. unsalted butter
1 tablespoon olive oil

Source: *The Cookery Year*, London: Readers Digest, 1973

It was all very tidy

When I reached his place
The grass was smooth
The wind was delicate
The wit well timed
The limbs well formed
The pictures straight on the wall
It was all very tidy

He was cancelling out
The last row of figures
He had his beard tied up in ribbons
There was no dust on his shoe
Everyone nodded
It was all very tidy

ROBERT GRAVES

General outlook

Fronts will move northeastwards across the British Isles. Northern Scotland and the northern isles will be cloudy and early on there will be sleet with snow on hills, some of it heavy.

Wales and the west of England will be cloudy with rain and drizzle at times, but will become clearer in the evening.

Eastern England will have drizzle in the morning. It may brighten up a little in the afternoon, but there will rain in the evening.

The west and north will be windy with gales, especially on coasts and hills, but temperatures will be well above average.

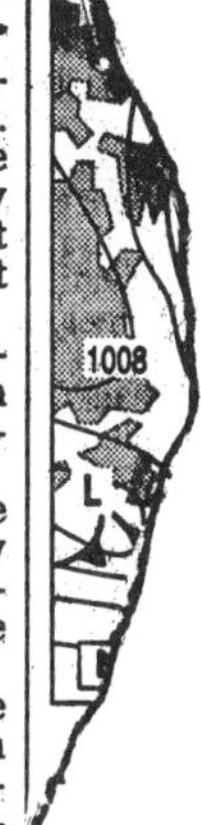

Source: *Guardian*, 17 February 1990

40 Transposition

Level	Advanced
Students	Teenage to adult, especially students of literature
Groups	Groups
Purpose	To show some of the differences between written and spoken English, notably in how they convey attitude and feeling
Text type	Thriller extract

In this activity

Learners prepare and perform a play scene based on a thriller extract, and then write the script.

Preparation

Find a thriller extract suitable for your learners — a sample is given in the material for this activity — and make one copy of it per learner.

In class

1. Divide the learners into groups and distribute copies of the thriller extract. Their task is to devise a mime which will tell the story of their text as accurately as possible. Sound effects are permissible, but NOT English words! They should prepare to act out this mime for the rest of the class.
2. When everyone is ready, choose two or three of the groups and invite them to perform their mime. Ask the rest of the class to say what is happening in the mimes, and to describe the feelings and attitudes of the characters.
3. Ask for volunteers to put words to the mimes.
4. Groups of learners now rewrite the thriller extract as a play script, conveying as much of the feeling and atmosphere of the original thriller as possible. These scripts can be acted out, if time permits.

Variation

The process can be done in reverse, i.e. a play script can be mimed, then rewritten as a narrative.

Link

Guess who and how (46) in the Vocabulary within Spoken Discourse section also explores the relationship between what is said and how it is said.

Teacher's diary

How did the learners react to this activity? Can you think of other activities which would involve your learners in exploring differences between spoken and written English?

Sample teaching material

'The dead man lay face-down on the white carpet, blood oozing from a wound on the crown of his head. It wasn't pretty but then murder never was. I stood looking at pictures on the wall, glasses in a cabinet, and books on a shelf. I looked at anything other than what was lying only five feet from me.

'Inspector Jack Steel came over muttering some greeting, and as I rather expected he might, began asking questions. What was I doing here? Had I been here long? Did I know anything about the murder? Was I a friend of the dead man? I answered all of these easily enough. I was simply working for him. I'd come over to talk about his missing brother. When I got here he had already been killed. Then Steel asked one more question just for fun. I stared at him as though he were stupid. Why would I murder my own client? I wasn't crazy.'

SECTION X

VOCABULARY WITHIN WRITTEN DISCOURSE

Introduction

There are four activities in this section:

41. Word hopscotch

42. Clozings

43. Tracing relationships

44. Instructions — who for?

The activities in this section are concerned with discourse, i.e. with large chunks of text, rather than with isolated words or sentences. Marking texts in various ways can help students' reference skills, while gapped texts of various types may be useful in combating the tendency of learners to guess wildly at meanings instead of using clues from the context. The conventional view of vocabulary is that it consists of 'content' words and 'grammar' words: looking at how words behave within texts shows us that some may be neither. They may be used to organise what is said, or they may serve to keep conversation going. In Activity 41, learners build up their own texts from isolated words, working from word form towards meaning content. The other activities have authentic texts as their starting point: Activity 42 reconstitutes text and thereby helps learners to pay attention to contextual cues. Activity 43 focuses on surface form, and in particular on reference and linking. Activity 44 focuses on the meaning of instructions and also on how audience and purpose affect how instructions are written. Activity 41 is a game which can be played at all levels, but the other activities are suitable for older and higher-level learners.

41 Word hopscotch

Level Elementary to advanced

Students All ages

Groups Groups

Purpose Variation 1: To encourage learners' creativity with known vocabulary
Variation 2: To increase learners' confidence in deciphering unknown words from context

Text type Students' stories, from teacher's wordlist

In this activity

Learners play a story-telling game based on words taken at random.

Preparation

You will need to work with words transcribed on to game boards, as in the sample teaching material for this activity. Nouns are simplest to work with for younger or lower-level learners. You will also need dice and counters.

In class

Variation 1

1. Divide the class into groups and distribute one game board per group, with two dice and a counter for each student.
2. Each learner in the group makes a dice throw. S/he can choose to use one or two dice. S/he makes the appropriate move, corresponding to the number thrown, and notes down the word s/he lands on.
3. As a group effort, learners construct a piece of writing to include the words they have landed on collectively. They check their work with the teacher.
4. Learners read out their stories to the other groups.

Variation 2

The procedure is the same except that the game board is made up of nonsense words. Learners follow Steps 1–3 as before, and the nonsense words can mean anything they choose. They then swop their stories with another group and write down what they think the nonsense words in the text are supposed to mean. In a whole class discussion, learners read aloud the texts they have worked on to the other groups and say how they arrived at their conclusions about the meanings of the nonsense words.

Further variation

Learners tell their stories, rather than write them. This is more difficult, and is more appropriate for advanced learners.

Link

Form-focused spelling puzzles (7) and **Sneaky spelling practice (9)** from the Sound–Spelling section, and **The affix game (21)** fron. the Word Grammar section are other self-contained gamelike activities.

Teacher's diary

Which variation did you try? How did the learners react to this activity? Would you change anything in the procedure for next time?

Sample teaching material

Game board for Word hopscotch, Variation 1:

1. DIAMOND	2. UNCLE	3. AFRAID	4. SKIES
5. CARPET	6. INDIA	7. CAMERA	8. MILLIONAIRE
9. JAIL	10. HOLE	11. JET	12. STORMY

Game board for Word hopscotch, Variation 2:

1. SQUORK	2. MUGGU	3. GACH	4. SPLOD
5. KRIJ	6. OLK	7. BLOIB	8. SKWISH
9. CHENG	10. AINOW	11. PRUGLE	12. ZOP

42 Clozings

Level Elementary to advanced

Students All ages

Groups Individual, pair or group

Purpose To give practice in using context to guess the meaning of unknown vocabulary items

Text type Teacher's texts

In this activity

Learners work on gapped or altered texts, towards reconstituting the original.

The following activities are based on the cloze principle of creating gaps in a text, which learners then reconstitute. Sample texts are given in the teaching material.

Variation 1: Part deletion

Instead of deleting whole words, delete parts of words. In this way, endings such as -ly, -ing, -ed, or beginnings such as dis-, un-, give learners valuable clues as to how the word is functioning within the given context. Alternatively, you can block out the top half or bottom half of the word, leaving clues to letter shape and sequence.

Variation 2: C-type

Instead of leaving the whole word blank, delete the second half of the word only, and indicate each letter deleted by a dash.

Variation 3: Wuggling

Instead of deleting words, substitute nonsense words which retain appropriate endings, thus providing grammatical clues.

Variation 4: Substitution

Instead of deleting words, underline ten to fifteen items which you think will be unknown, and provide a jumbled list of synonyms for learners to substitute.

Variation 5: Suggestopedic*

Present the text in its entirety first, then take it in again and give out another text identical to the first except for a few items, for which you have substituted erroneous items. Learners try to replace these with the originals.

Variation 6: Learner version

Students create their own deletions from a given text and swop texts with other learners.

Link

This activity revises and extends work from the Collocation section, especially **A bottle of beer (22)**.

Teacher's diary

Which activity did you try? How did the learners react? Were any of the items more difficult to guess than you had predicted?

Sample teaching material

1. Part deletion

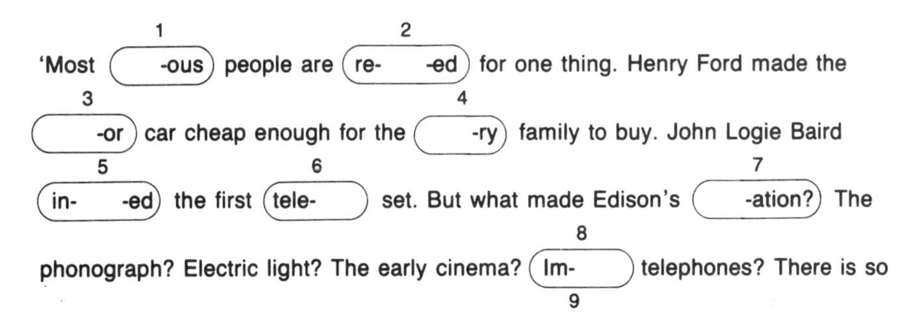

'Most (1 -ous) people are (2 re- -ed) for one thing. Henry Ford made the (3 -or) car cheap enough for the (4 -ry) family to buy. John Logie Baird (5 in- -ed) the first (6 tele-) set. But what made Edison's (7 -ation?) The phonograph? Electric light? The early cinema? (8 Im-) telephones? There is so

9

* Suggestopedia is an approach to teaching which was devised by Georgi Lozanov, whose work is mentioned in the Reference section.

much to choose from. There are hundreds of (-ents) in Edison's name; he

10 11

kept on (-ing) for more than (-ty) years.'

2. C-type

'He looked up at me. And I had a terr– – – – surprise. The man was Prof– – – – – Wexford. But he was only ju– – Prof– – – – – Wexford. He had changed. It was a terr– – – – change. I hadn't seen him for th– – – years. That was when he sto– – – – work — ret– – – – from the unive– – – – – –.'

3. Wuggling

'Last Saturday, I went WUGGLING in Sheffield. I wanted to buy some WUGGLES for my family for Christmas. First, I went to a clothes shop and bought a WUGGLE for my father. I chose a furry one with flaps to keep his ears warm. Next, I went to choose some WUGGLERY for my sister. I found a beautiful locket of silver with a matching chain. I do hope my family will be WUGGLY when they see what I have bought.'

4. Substitution

'The aircraft of the R.A.F. are always well serviced. The men who look after them are called fitters and mechanics. The crew of an aircraft use a lot of electronic equipment. Some of it keeps them in contact with men and equipment on the ground. Warning lights let the crew know if any parts of the aircraft are not working properly. Skilled men check all of this equipment.

Air crews have to wear special clothes when they are flying. Fighter pilots sit in seats that can be catapulted out of the aircraft if it is going to crash. All aircrews have parachutes, and these must be checked to make sure that they work properly if needed . . .'

Match words underlined with one of the following synonyms:

RECEIVE	REQUIRED	EJECTED FROM	TRANSMIT
TRAINED	MAINTAIN	TAKEN WITH	ACCURATE

5. Suggestopedic

'"Don't speak to me like that!" he barked.

'Sam threw up his hands: "Hey! Aren't you being a bit unfair? There's no

1

need to be umbrageous just because I told you to change your clothes. You want

to get this job, don't you?"

'"Well of course I do," Harry snapped, more subdued now.

2
'"Well then, you slubberdegullion, don't you think it's worth wearing a decent suit for the interview?"

3
'Harry manducated his rump steak for a moment or two and then said, simply: " I don't have a decent suit. I don't have a suit at all, as a matter of fact."'

Key:
1. huffy, 2. chump, 3. chewed

43 Tracing relationships

Level	Intermediate to advanced
Students	Adults
Groups	Individuals
Purpose	To sensitise learners to some of the factors contributing to cohesion in English
Text type	Teacher's chosen text, or students' written work

In this activity

Learners annotate their own written work in order to increase their understanding of vocabulary for reference and linking.

Preparation

Find a text which is appropriate in level for your class, or use a reformulated piece of learner's written work. The sample teaching material for this activity is a reformulated learner text produced in answer to the question, 'Can men and women ever be equal?' The teacher, instead of correcting it, rewrote it, keeping as much of the original as possible. Reformulating learners' work in this way often shows up factors which would not be revealed through normal error-correction techniques, such as reference and linking words.

In class

Choose shapes which you will use to signal types of relationship: the sample shows an oval shape for 'reference' and a rectangle for 'linking'. Draw in these shapes on your text, in colour if possible, according to whichever of the following variations you wish to use:

Variation 1

Draw the appropriate shape around reference words and have learners trace them back to their referent.

Variation 2

Underline appropriate words in the text, and have learners themselves draw in the appropriate shape around them.

Variation 3

Draw shapes around appropriate words, but also delete some of the words within these shapes for learners to guess.

The sample teaching material for this activity shows a combination of Variations 1 and 3. It brings home to the learners the importance of clarity — 'their' in line two is ambiguous as to its referent, as shown.

Link

It might be appropriate to use this activity with **Playing the top ten (31)** from the Frequency section.

Teacher's diary

How did the learners react to this activity? Did it help them to use more reference and linking words in their writing?

Sample teaching material

Learner's reformulated text:

'For many years, people have been interested in the difference between men and women, and in the effect this has on their abilities. Some believe that there are many points of difference, 1 others believe there are few. Who is correct?

'All through the centuries there have been certain societies dominated by women and others dominated by men: both systems seem to have worked equally well, if we consider the examples of Cleopatra and of Julius Caesar. Did sex have any importance there?

'We live in an age in which people worry about such matters. Perhaps they worry because they have nothing better to do with their time. We are part of a society in which both women and men can achieve the same standards. This is a happy state of affairs. [2], I do not think we should attach much importance to the subject of equality of the sexes.

'[3], I would state my own opinion, which is that men and women can achieve equality in those areas to which mental, rather than physical, factors are relevant.'

Key:
1. while, whilst, 2. however, 3. finally

44 Instructions — who for?

Level	Upper intermediate to advanced, especially ESP learners
Students	Adults
Groups	Individual, pairs or groups
Purpose	To show the importance of keeping 'audience' and 'purpose' in mind, when writing instructions
Text type	Teacher's authentic extracts from instruction manuals

In this activity

Learners work on a random set of instructions, to discover who they were written for, and why.

Preparation

Assemble sets of instructions and mount on card. Samples are given as teaching material for this activity. Post them around the walls of the classroom.

In class

1. Ask your learners, working in pairs or groups, to skim-read the extracts and say who they think each one was written for. Ask them to note down, as they do so, the words or phrases which helped them arrive at an answer.
2. Bring the class together to discuss how they came to their decisions.
3. Write on the board or overhead projector the words and phrases which provided clues about who the instructions were for. Ask which instructions could be spoken and which only read? Why? (e.g. long sentences: 'melt the chocolate in a bowl over a pan of hot water and with the aid of two forks, dip the dates in the chocolate'; passive constructions: 'he or she may be tilted back, the seat carefully slid out and the legs laid flat').
4. Hand out the list of sources so that learners can check whether their guesses were correct.

Link

Photofits (37) or **Transposition (40)** from the Register section are other activities which focus on differences between written and spoken English.

Teacher's diary

How did your learners react to this activity? Which texts did they find most difficult? Why? Are there other types of instructions which you could use?

Sample teaching material

A.

After the cables have been drawn in fix all covers in position.

Ensure that the conduit is neat in appearance.

Keep bends and sets to standard radii and angles.

Keep the number of bends and sets to a minimum.

FYT Booklet No. 11, *Training Practice for First Year Trainees in Electrical Engineering*, Engineering Industry Training Board, 1979

B.

1. Be sure that all loose clothing is tucked in to prevent it from becoming caught by the revolving work.
2. Cover the lathe bed with paper (Fig. 10-34).
3. Set the lathe at a high speed and disengage the lead screw and feed rod.
4. Mount work between centres freely with very little end play, or use a rotating dead centre.
5. Use a piece of 80 to 100 grit abrasive cloth about 25 mm wide for rough polishing.
6. Hold the abrasive cloth as shown in Figure 10-34 to prevent the top end of the abrasive cloth from wrapping around the work and injuring the fingers.

7. Hold the long end of the abrasive cloth *securely* with one hand while the fingers of the other hand press the cloth against the diameter (Fig. 10-34).
8. Slowly move the abrasive cloth back and forth along the diameter to be polished.

Krar, S.F. and St Amand, J.E., *Machine Shop Training*, 3rd edn, McGraw Hill, 1977

C.

Routine maintenance should include the following:

Washing
Road grit and mud should be removed by frequent washing of the paintwork. Very careful attention should be given to out-of-sight areas such as beneath the sills, bottom of door jambs and other places where corrosion starts.

Polishing
Periodic wax polishing protects the paintwork and improves the appearance. Brightwork should also be polished to seal the small scratches.

Hillier, V. *Motor Vehicle Basic Principles*, Hutchinsons, 1979

D.

Occasionally, circumstances may justify cutting the seat mounts and removing the victim on the seat. He or she may then be tilted back to lie on a stretcher, the seat carefully slid out and the legs laid flat. A patient should not be left sitting upright if shocked, but otherwise could be taken to the hospital on the seat.

Book 12 of *Practical Firemanship 11*, Chapter 6, Home Office, 1983

SECTION XI

VOCABULARY WITHIN SPOKEN DISCOURSE

Introduction

There are six activities in this section:

45. I got rhythm

46. Guess who and how

47. Overstating and understating

48. Over and over again

49. Organising discourse

50. English as she is spoke

In spoken communication, there are many factors, other than the literal meaning of the words used, which help us to understand what we hear. They include gesture and facial expression, as well as intonation, stress and pausing. There are certain words which are commonly used to indicate beginnings and endings of sections of discourse, and speakers also help their hearers by repeating information — either by summarising what they have just said, or by rephrasing it. Many of the words we use in conversation have little semantic content, but are there to maintain interaction between speaker and hearer.

The activities in this section cover all the aspects of spoken discourse which have just been outlined. Activity 45 is concerned with sentence stress and its relationship to weak vowels in English. It gives learners a way of holding in memory those half-heard words which cause problems for comprehension. Activity 46 uses video to show how attitude can be expressed other than through word meanings alone. Activity 47 shows some of the ways English speakers soften the impact of what they say, and also how they emphasise what is important. Activity 48 gives learners practice in repeating identical information in different ways — a feature of spoken English which they, in their turn, need to appreciate when they listen to spoken English. Activity 49 is concerned with discourse organisers: the words and phrases English speakers use to structure what they say, so that their hearers can follow the message easily. Finally, Activity 50 focuses on the features of English pronunciation which can help learners understand speech delivered at speed.

45 I got rhythm

Level Elementary to advanced, depending on input

Students All ages

Groups Pairs and whole class

Purpose To train learners to listen for cues related to stress patterns in English, in order to help understanding of English spoken at native speed

Text type Teacher's text

In this activity

Learners use dictation as a vehicle for training their ears to 'sound shapes'.

Variation 1

English is often described as a 'stress timed' language, i.e. one having regular beats, or strong stresses, interspersed with weak stresses. It is the weakly stressed words, which are often the little 'grammar' words like 'the', 'then', 'it' and so on, which tend to be missed by foreign learners. Here are three ways of practising listening for these weakly stressed items:

1. Dictate a text, but provide learners with the text to be dictated *minus* all the 'grammatical' words. A sample is given as teaching material for this activity.
2. Learners work in pairs to dictate to each other. One partner dictates the text, and the other has to listen for an agreed 'grammar word' such as an article or preposition. Each time this word appears, the listener rings a bell/claps hands, or gives some other agreed signal that the word has been heard.
3. Tell your learners that you are going to dictate a text, and that they are to count how many times a given 'grammar' word appears. After the activity, check answers with copies of the original text.

Variation 2

It can be helpful for learners to have some way of recording the 'sound shape' of a word they have heard but not understood. The system I use for this is a dot for a weak stress and a dash for a strong stress, i.e. the words 'carefully' and 'disappointing' would be represented respectively as: —.. and ..—. It is easy to use this method of notation at speed, during a lecture or talk, and in this way learners have a 'sound clue' to the word they missed, so that they have a better chance of working out what must have been said. Here is a way of training learners to be aware of word stress:

Dictate a text for which you provide learners with a gapped version. For each gap, instead of dictating the original word, you dictate a nonsense word which preserves the number and duration of syllables in the original, as well as its stress pattern, e.g. 'A new phone book will be DIDADEE this week to DADIDEE subscribers in the town' (from the sample teaching material for this activity). This technique is especially good for alerting learners to the shifting stress in context of multisyllabic words, such as 'disappointing', 'everlasting', 'underneath'. Compare 'a disappointing result', 'to his everlasting credit', 'he was underneath the bedclothes.'

Link

This is a spoken version of **Clozings (42)** from the Vocabulary within Written Discourse section. **Syllable snap (8)** from the Sound–Spelling section would be a good warm-up activity for this one.

Teacher's diary

Were learners able to use the shorthand system proposed for Variation 2? Did Variation 1 help them to catch more of the grammatical words in spoken English?

Sample teaching material

Variation 1 a): *'New telephone directory*

— new phone book — — delivered — week — telephone subscribers — — town. — look — changed. — phone book now — — light blue cover — — line drawing — — fountain — Central Square.'

Key: a/will/be/this/to/in/the/the/has/the/has/a/with/a/of/the/in

46 Guess who and how

Level Elementary to advanced, depending on input

Students All ages

Groups Pairs or groups

Purpose To sensitise learners to the relationship between *what* is said and *how* it is said

Text type Teacher's video clip(s)

In this activity

Learners act out a scene, based on a video soundtrack, and then compare it with the original.

A common technique for exploiting video in class is to turn down the soundtrack of a picture sequence and to invite learners to supply the missing dialogue, using clues from paralinguistic features, dress, expression and so on. The following activity reverses the process.

Preparation

Assemble snippets of video suitable for the activity, i.e. extracts showing different situations and different relationships between protagonists, e.g. boss/employee, mother/child, boyfriend/girlfriend, etc.

In class

1. Either play the soundtrack without the picture, or supply written transcripts of the video clip(s) for learners to read silently.
2. Elicit from learners their ideas on the sex, age, dress, attitude, expression, relationship of the protagonists.

3. Invite a few learners to act out the scene, using appropriate gestures and facial expressions. Video this acting if possible.
4. Finally, show the original clip(s), for comparison, and discuss differences between it/them and the class members' versions.

Link

Experiencing is knowing (16) from the Denotation section is another activity which explores the relationship between what is said and how it is said.

Teacher's diary

How did the learners react to this activity? Were there large differences between the original scene(s) and your learners' performances?

47 Overstating and understating

Level Intermediate and advanced

Students Adults

Groups Individuals or groups

Purpose To aquaint learners with some of the ways of 'downgrading' and 'emphasising' in English, and to encourage learners to experiment for themselves

Text type Teacher's situational dialogues

In this activity

Learners add to dialogues in order to soften or to emphasise their message, then act them out.

'Downgraders' are words and phrases used to soften the impact of what we want to say, when it is in danger of being surprising or offensive to our hearer, e.g. if asked 'You don't like him, do you?', we might say, 'Well, I do, as a matter of fact.' 'Well' and 'as a matter of fact' soften the impact of the answer. We could have said, 'in a way' or 'I'm afraid to say' instead.

'Emphasisers' are words and phrases used to highlight parts of what we want to say, so that we can make an impact on our hearer, e.g. 'absolutely' in the phrase, 'It was absolutely superb' would be an 'emphasiser'. Others include auxiliary verbs, e.g. 'I do believe', 'He will insist', adjectives of positive or negative bias, e.g. 'sheer delight', 'a hopeless muddle', and repetition, e.g. 'She wants to talk and talk'.

Preparation

Use the sample material for this activity. It gives one exercise for 'downgraders' and one for 'emphasisers', with possible solutions.

In class

1. Give groups of learners your situations and/or set of utterances, after giving them an example or two, perhaps from the introduction to this activity.
2. Invite learners to work together to discuss possible solutions.
3. Invite some of the learners to act out what they have decided for the situations, and read out what they have decided for the utterances, before distributing the key.

Link

The activity **Guess who and how (46)** which precedes this one, is a useful companion to it.

Teacher's diary

How did your learners react to this activity? Did it throw up any cultural differences — were some learners accustomed to being more/less direct than is usual in English?

Sample teaching material

Downgraders:

In each situation below, you are given a bald statement to say. Discuss how you could add to this statement without changing any of the words within it, so as to 'soften the blow':

1. A very dear friend of yours has just bought some new clothes and is very pleased with them. You don't like them:
   FRIEND: How do you like my new outfit? It's the first time I've worn it.
   YOU: I think it's awful.
2. You have arranged to meet an old friend tonight at the cinema but you now realise that you have overlooked a previous engagement. You meet by chance in the street during the day:
   FRIEND: Well, hello there! I'm really looking forward to tonight.
   YOU: I can't come.
3. Your boss wants to have an 'open day' to show the kind of work done in the

establishment in which you work. You have no desire to run it. On the contrary, you have told your boss that you will do so only if no one else can be found to take it on:

BOSS: What are the arrangements for the open day? You said you would get your department to organise it.

YOU: No I didn't.

4. You and your friend are part of a team working on a new project. A mutual colleague has been chosen to lead it. You do not share your friend's opinion about this colleague, but you want to avoid an argument:

   FRIEND: S/he's absolutely impossible to work with! What's more, s/he's just plain incompetent.

   YOU: I think s/he's the ideal person for the job.

Key:

(One native speaker's response)

1. Well, if you really want to know, I think it's awful.
2. Well actually, I'm frightfully sorry, but I can't come.
3. No I didn't, in fact.
4. I think s/he's the ideal person for the job, if you want my honest opinion.

Emphasisers:

Here are some ways speakers may use to emphasise what they say. Discuss other ways they could have achieved the same effect. The 'emphasiser' has been underscored for you in each case, and you should replace it with another of your own, e.g.:

There was quite a large input — The amount of input was pretty large.

1. But it's inevitable, isn't it?
2. This is a very important question.
3. We try to make our voice heard as loudly as possible.
4. Only a handful of people know we exist.
5. What I'm really concerned about is that we should appeal to everyone.
6. Well, there are training units nationally, but not necessarily locally.
7. Most of us thoroughly enjoy our work.

Key:

(One native speaker's response)

1. But it's inevitable, that's obvious.
2. This is a terribly important question.
3. We try to make our voice heard as well as we can.
4. A mere handful of people know we exist.
5. What I'm concerned about above all is that we should . . .
6. Well there are training units nationally of course, but . . .
7. Most of us enjoy our work tremendously.

48 Over and over again

Level Intermediate to advanced

Students Teenage to adult

Groups Variation 1: groups as teams; Variation 2: pairs or groups

Purpose To show learners the value of repetition when communicating in English, and to give practice in saying the same thing in different ways

Text type Teacher's prompts

In this activity

Learners play a game in which they repeat identical information using a different form of words.

We repeat ourselves when we speak; this is part of the redundancy of the spoken language. People do this for two main reasons: to ensure that they have been understood, and to keep conversation going.

Variation 1

In English, if you simply answer a question with 'Yes' or 'No', this is not enough to sound interested and leave the way open for further conversation. It is better to reply by saying the same thing in a different way, e.g.:

'Lovely day, isn't it?'

'Yes, beautiful' or 'Yes, wonderful'.

Here is a team game to practise this:

Preparation

Write suitable questions on scraps of paper. Samples are given in the material for this activity. Depending on level, you can allow your learners to see these questions in advance of the game, or not.

In class

The first member of Team A picks a question and asks it of a nominated member of Team B, who responds appropriately, e.g. to the question, 'Lovely day isn't it?' s/he responds, 'Yes, beautiful'. Another member of Team B makes a further response, e.g. 'Yes, gorgeous', a third member of Team B gives another response, and so on until all of Team B have responded or until they run out of ideas for responses. The turn then passes to Team B, who ask the next question of Team A, and so on. Each appropriate response gains one point. The game ends when all questions have been asked.

Variation 2

The procedure is similar to Variation 1, but the game can be played in pairs. Instead of questions, statements are made, which have to be paraphrased, e.g. A's statement could be, 'I've got two sisters' and B's response could be, 'I see, so there are two girls in your family besides yourself.'

Follow-up

Find authentic English monologues and ask your learners to find places where the speakers repeat themselves. The best way of working on this is to provide transcripts for learners to mark.

Link

This activity complements the previous one, **Overstating and understating (47)**.

Teacher's diary

Which variation did you choose? How did the learners react? Would you change anything in the procedure for next time?

Sample teaching material

Variation 1: Questions

1. Lovely day, isn't it?
2. Horrid weather isn't it?
3. That woman's so elegant, don't you think?
4. Have you given up cigarettes?

5. They say she's expecting twins.
6. I do hate this game don't you?

Key: Some native speaker responses

1. Yes, beautiful/wonderful/gorgeous.
2. Yes, foul/ghastly/revolting.
3. Yes, she moves beautifully/such taste!/what dress sense!
4. Yes, I never touch them now/completely/I don't smoke at all now.
5. Yes, just imagine — two at once/double trouble/two of them.
6. Yes, I can't stand it/loathe it/absolutely detest it.

49 Organising discourse

Level Advanced

Students Adults

Groups Individual, pairs or groups

Purpose To raise learners' awareness of how speakers organise what they say, in order to facilitate understanding. To improve learners' own ability to organise discourse

Text type Teacher's transcript of authentic spoken English

In this activity

Learners discover discourse organisers from authentic spoken English, to help them when preparing their own presentations.

'Discourse organisers' can be classified into three types: (a) those that focus on what will follow; (b) those that sum up or focus on what has been said; and (c) those that form a boundary between what has been said and what will come next. Look at the sample teaching material for this activity for illustrations of each.

Preparation

It will be more appropriate for your learners if you make tape recordings of native speakers whom they know. You will need to transcribe these, underline the discourse organisers, and make copies of the extracts. Alternatively, use the sample material for this activity.

In class

1. Ask your learners for any thoughts they may have on what makes it easy for them to follow an English speaker who is explaining something. Have they noticed any expressions you yourself use, e.g. 'I mean', 'The thing is . . .', 'Now . . .'.

2. Give out copies of your transcript and invite learners to work in groups to classify the discourse organisers you have underlined according to categories (a), (b) and (c) above. A sample is given.
3. After an appropriate time, bring the learners together as a whole class to check answers.
4. Repeat the procedure with other extracts. With advanced learners, you could present the second extract 'cold', i.e. unmarked, so that learners themselves have to find examples of the three types of discourse organiser. A further sample is given for this, as suggested in the material for this activity.
5. Invite your learners to work on their own presentations, incorporating appropriate 'organisers'.

Link

Overstating and understating (47) from this section gives learners additional help for preparing oral presentations.

Teacher's diary

How did the learners react to this activity? Were they able to improve the organisation of their own presentations as a result?

Sample teaching material

Transcript with discourse organisers underscored:

'"Can you tell me what you mean by 'stress'?"

'"What I mean by 'stress' is when pressure exceeds an individual's ability to cope with it. In other words, pressure is usually fairly healthy, it stimulates people to action, but when that pressure gets to the point that you get maladaptive behaviour in one form or another, either social behaviour that's not appropriate, or health behaviour, it affects your health, your relationships, your marriage, then I think we're moving from pressure into stress."

'"I see, And how does stress counselling work?"

'"I think its very important that management should know the kind of pressures involved for the people they are employing and should do something to help. Stress counselling is nothing more than a service made available by trained staff whereby any member of staff can go in if they have a problem. Now the problem does not have to be a work-related problem. The object of that is, if an individual is having a problem in his marriage, that person is going to walk into work and that problem's not going to go away, it's going to affect him or her at work. So basically the service really allows an individual to go for help, somebody to talk to. It may be a long-term problem or a legal problem that requires more expertise, in which case that person can then be referred."

'"How does this service differ from others already in existence?"

'"OK. What we've done is we've carried out a systematic evaluation and we've found substantial drops in anxiety levels, depression levels and psychosomatic symptoms. But more interesting than that is that we looked at what happened in the workplace. These counsellors are not only concerned with the individual but with the organisation. And we found between a 50 and 60 per cent decline in sickness absence over a six-month period. So it'll save the organisation quite a lot of money."

Key:

(a) type organisers: I think it's very important that . . .
. . . nothing more than . . .
What we've done is . . .
But more interesting than that is . . .

(b) type organisers: In other words . . .
So basically . . .
So . . .

(c) type organisers: Now . . .
OK . . .

Further sample material

Use the extract given as teaching material for **English as she is spoke (50)** for which the key is as follows:

Type (a) organisers: Line 1 : 'You know'
Line 11: 'a couple', which leads on to 'one' (line 12), 'The next one' (line 15), 'the next one' (line 19)

Type (b) organisers: Line 1 : 'so'
Line 25: 'so'
Line 26: 'so'

Type (c) organisers: Line 3 : 'OK'
Line 8 : 'so'?
Line 11: 'so'
Line 26: 'OK'
Line 30: 'Right'

It is worth noting how this speaker sequences the discourse, making it doubly easy to follow the line of argument, namely:

Line 8: 'It starts off'
Line 9: 'and then she goes on'
Line 10: 'and at the end'
Line 11: 'First of all'
Line 24: 'And finally'
Line 27: 'And now'

50 English as she is spoke

Level Advanced

Students Adults

Groups Individuals, pairs or groups

Purpose To train learners to hear and be aware of some of the most common contractions, assimilations and elisions common in English spoken at speed

Text type Teacher's authentic extracts of spoken English

In this activity

Learners work on isolated examples of some features of spoken English, before looking at the same features in discourse.

Variation 1: Looking at contractions

Preparation

Make a transcript of a piece of authentic spoken English and underline the contractions. Samples are given in the material for this activity.

In class

Invite learners to look at the transcript and decide what the full form of the contractions would be. Alternatively, they could work on a written text and discuss where contractions might occur if the text were spoken.

Variation 2: Looking at assimilations

Preparation

Initial consonants usually retain their true value in English speech, but these consonants often merge into the following sounds when they occur at the ends of words. This is especially true for /t/, /d/ and /n/. Find some examples of this feature, or use the samples given for this activity.

In class

1. Invite learners to read aloud the examples you have chosen, in order to discover how the word or phrase should really be spelled.
2. Next, invite learners to examine a transcript of authentic spoken English for places where similar processes might be at work. A sample is given in the material for this activity.

Variation 3: Looking at elisions

Preparation

Sometimes, especially at the ends of words, consonants are missed out altogether. In fact, this is so common with /d/ and /t/ as to be the norm for spoken English. Find some examples of this feature, or use the samples given for this activity.

In class

1. Invite your learners to read aloud the examples you have chosen, and decide how each word or phrase should really be spelled.
2. Invite learners to examine an authentic spoken text, and discover places where the feature might occur. A sample text is given in the material for this activity.

Variation 4: Looking for weak vowels

Preparation

Vowels often disappear in multisyllabic words, where there is weak stress. Find examples of words having this feature, or use the sample material for this activity.

In class

1. Invite learners to read your examples aloud, as though the vowels in question were missing altogether. Samples are given in the material for this activity.
2. Invite learners to look for this feature in an authentic spoken text. Alternatively, they could mark a written text for places where the feature might occur if the text were spoken. An authentic spoken text is given in the material for this activity.

Link

Form-focused spelling puzzles (7) or **How do I say it? (11)** from the Sound–Spelling section are other activities which are concerned with pronunciation.

Teacher's diary

Which variation did you try? How did the learners react to this activity? Was it difficult to convince learners that the feature in fact exists in spoken English?

Sample teaching material

Variation 1:

'The accused man defended himself. 'I'm not a bad man, Your Honour,' he said. 'I've just got to see a dog and I'm thinking how to catch it. It's so easy really. You've got a packet of crisps in your pocket and you rustle it a bit. The dog's got a nose and an ear. And he's interested. Next thing you know, he'll be walking down the road behind you."'

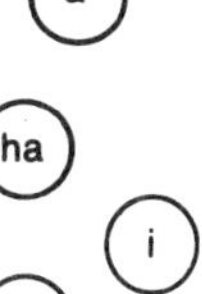

Variation 2:

1. GrapeBritain 2. Stapement 3. Hundrebpounds 4. Iwongkgo
5. Armourgcar 6. Ivebeengconcentrating.

Key:
Great Britain/Statement/Hundred pounds/I won't go/Armoured car/I've been concentrating

Variation 3:

1. Firsthree 2. Lasyear 3. WesGerman 4. Aspecs 5. Thefacthat
6. Asconfuseasever 7. NorthernIrelantroubles 9. Nothingstanstill

Key:
First three/Last year/West German/Aspects/The fact that/As confused as ever/ Northern Ireland troubles/Nothing stands still

Variation 4:

1. Intrest 2. Diffrent 3. Cllective 4. Pliticl 5. Cabnet
6. Chancllor 7. Simlar 8. Libry 9. Secrtry 10. Govnor
11. Medcne

Key:
Interest/Different/Collective/Political/Cabinet/Chancellor/
Similar/Library/Secretary/Governor/Medicine

Authentic Spoken Texts

1. Knock-knock jokes: these can be the subject of a problem-solving activity, as learners try to discover what the punchline means:

   (a) — 'Knock knock' — 'Who's there?' — 'Jemimah' — 'Jemimah who?' — 'Jemimah coming in? It's cold outside'
   (Do you mind my coming in? . . .)

   (b) — 'Knock knock' — 'Who's there?' — 'Juno' — 'Juno who?'
   — 'Juno your house is on fire?' (Do you know your house . . .)

   (c) — 'Knock knock' — 'Who's there?' — 'Nelly' — 'Nelly who?'
   — 'Nelly midnight, Cinderella' (Nearly midnight . . .)

2. Authentic native English speaker's presentation transcript, marked for the features mentioned in Variations 1 to 4. Contractions are underscored, elisions and weak vowels are shown by deletions, and assimilations are shown by linking and superscript:

   '"You know we've been^m busy lately with er organising our students for our student^m profile. Yeah? So we've been busy with student needs. OK. The article I'm going to talk about takes that . . . takes that a step further. It's concerned more with student expectations. Expectations as to what^k good teaching is and^m beliefs as to how they learn. And the title of the article, if I can remember it, is "Helping Language Learners Think about Learning". So it starts off; she illustrates a couple of basic beliefs about training and then she goes on to give some practical ideas, some practical activities, and at the end she just talks about the value of this. So first of all she has a couple of little case studies. One is Miguel, whom we've read about. Yeah? And^m Miguel learns naturally, you know? He likes to communicate and he sees it^p more as an unconscious process. Maybe you could say it's just like Krashen's acquisition. The next one is a learner from South Korea and she believes that learning systematically is the best way. She has to understand the way the language works before she can use it. For her it's a conscious process. Yeah?

She learns best that way. Then the next sort of case study she gives brings up other factors and these are more affective factors. The self concept of the learner. Yeah? You know, 'Am I a good learner or am I stupid?" "All the other kids are more clever than I am." It's also the em beliefs as to how one learns. And finally — not finally, but also — whether you like the teacher. Hm? All these things are affective factors. So these sort of go right across the scale. OK. So this is the scenario we have. And now she puts forward a few ideas, a few practical activities, and these activities are really humanistic activities. Yeah? They encourage the learner to examine the beliefs and the self concepts and past experience. Right . . ."'

POSTSCRIPT

Wholebrained vocabulary acquisition

The activities in this book have focused variously on 'form', e.g. spelling or word formation, and on 'content', e.g. denotative and connotative meaning. Below is a technique for connecting the two: for marrying knowledge about a word with practical experience of using it for communicating.

Level Elementary to advanced, depending on input

Students All ages

Groups Whole class, pairs or individuals

Purpose To improve memorisation of new vocabulary by engaging the whole person, physical, mental, auditory and visual

Text type Teacher's theme-based wordlist and text, visual aids

In this activity

Learners work through a series of tasks, from single words taken out of context towards using these words in connected discourse.

Preparation

The illustration I have chosen for this technique is for elementary ESP learners and is on the topic of 'the car', but following a recipe, arranging flowers, horse riding and many other topic areas lend themselves to similar treatment. Whichever you choose, you will need to prepare both a 'classroom' phase, with wall chart, labels, models and/or diagrams, video if available, and a 'hands-on' phase, which will provide an opportunity for learners to use the vocabulary from the 'classroom' phase.

In class

1. Show the class a model car and ask learners to volunteer any item of motoring vocabulary they know. Make sure you teach 'seatbelt', 'mirror', 'clutch', 'pedal', 'accelerator', 'gear lever', 'handbrake' and 'ignition', if these are not volunteered.
2. Invite your learners to practise the new vocabulary by pointing to the relevant

car parts on your model, as you pass it around. If you have enough models available, learners can work in pairs on this simultaneously.

3. Display a wall chart showing a car. Deal out card labels on which you have written some of the vocabulary for parts of a car, including a few which you have not mentioned.
4. Invite learners to come to the chart and label it, using their cards. Check that the labels have been placed correctly.
5. Tell your learners that they are to imagine themselves in the role of driving instructor, and produce a sequence of instructions which will allow a learner driver to move off from a stationary position. Discuss these instructions with them orally. You will probably find you need to supply verbs such as 'switch on', 'adjust', 'depress', 'release', 'signal' 'fasten'. Invite individual learners to repeat the necessary sequence of actions.
6. Give each learner a sentence from Step 5. Invite learners to record these sentences in sequence so that a complete class recording of driving instructions results. Ten instructions is a manageable number, so some learners may not get a turn at recording, unless you make several recordings from which you choose the clearest or most accurate.
7. Take the learners outside to your car — or to a learner's car. Pick one learner to act as driver. Insert the cassette tape into the car cassette recorder. The 'driver' must follow the instructions s/he hears, with the help of other learners as necessary.
8. Repeat the process with other learners taking the part of 'driver'. Then, without the cassette, invite one learner to take the role of 'instructor' and give instructions verbally to a 'driver'.

Link

Which sense? (27) from the Polysemy section is another activity which moves from decontextualised work to using the same vocabulary in context.

Teacher's diary

Which topic area did you use for this activity? What was the reaction of your learners? Were they able to use the vocabulary they had practised in the classroom phase?

Notes and references

The reader's attention is drawn to the **Further Reading** section in the Introduction to this book, which gives short synopses of books for teachers and learners which are specifically related to vocabulary. Below is a list of other works which have been consulted or used as illustrations for this book, in order of appearance (other sources have been acknowledged elsewhere):

Introduction

Donley, M., 'The role of structural semantics in expanding and activating the vocabulary of the advanced learner: the example of the homophone', *Audio Visual Language Journal*, **12**, 2 (1974): 81–9.

Henning, G., 'Remembering foreign language vocabulary acoustic and semantic parameters', *Language Learning*, **23**, 2 (1973): 185–95.

Mother tongue

C.E. Ott, D.C. Butler, R.S. Blake and J.P. Ball, 'The effect of interactive image elaboration on the acquisition of foreign language vocabulary', *Language Learning*, **23**, 2 (1973): 197–206.

McDowell, J. and Hart, C., *Listening Plus*, Unit 13, London: Arnold, 1987.

Hartley, B. and Viney, P., *Streamline English Destinations*, London: Oxford University Press, 1982.

Sound–Spelling

Gattegno, C., *Teaching Foreign Languages in Schools: The Silent Way*, 2nd edn, Reading: Educational Solutions, 1972.

Gattegno, C., *The Common Sense of Teaching Foreign Languages*, Reading: Educational Solutions, 1976.

Denotation

Heidenhain, G., 'Drama activities in the suggestopedic language classroom', Proceedings of the 3rd International Conference of SEAL (unpub.), 1989.

Word grammar

Kreidler, C., *The Pronunciation of English*, Oxford: Basil Blackwell, 1989.

Frequency

Hanks, P., 'How common is common?', in *Collins Dictionary Diary*, Glasgow: Collins, 1989.

Connotation

Kelly, G., (1955) 'The psychology of personal constructs', in Ewen, R., ed., *An Introduction to Theories of Personality*, 2nd edn, London: Academic Press, 1984.

Maley, A. and Duff, A. *Sounds Interesting* and *Sounds Intriguing*, London: Oxford University Press, 1984.
Willis, D. and Willis, J. *Cobuild English Course*, Book 2, 1989.

Register

Holden, S. (ed.) *Teaching Children*, London: Modern English Publications, 1980.
Swales, J., 'A genre based approach to language across the curriculum', paper delivered at 1985 RELC Conference.
Swales, J., 'Aspects of article introductions', Aston Research Reports, Jno. 1, University of Aston in Birmingham, 1981, p. 10.

Vocabulary within written discourse

Border, R., *Five Great Inventors*, Macmillan Range 6 Reader, London: Macmillan, 1978.
Victor, Paul (1979) *The Spy and Other Stories*, Longman Structural Reader, Stage 3, Harlow: Longman, 1979.
Lozanov, G. and Gateva, E., *The Foreign Language Teacher's Suggestopedic Manual*, London: Gordon Breach, 1988.

Vocabulary within spoken discourse

ALBSU/BBC *Switch on to English*, 1985.
The Collins/University of Birmingham Database of English Text
Carter, R. and McCarthy, M., *Vocabulary in Language Teaching*, Harlow: Longman, 1988.
Brown, G., *Listening to Spoken English* (2nd edn), Harlow: Longman, 1990.
Smart Alec's Knock Knock Jokes for Kids (1987) London: Ward Lock.
Rogers, J. *The Crazy Joke Book Strikes Back*, Beaver Books, 1985.
Needle, J. (ed.) *We are the Champions*, Piccolo, 1984.

INDEXES

A: Summary of activities

(NB: Activities are listed sequentially by section)

I: Mother tongue Equivalence

1. *Marks on a paper* (p.14) Learners guess meanings of unknown words written in various languages
2. *Key words* (p.16) Learners improve retention of word meanings by making visual, auditory or other associations
3. *What did you call me?* (p.18) Learners discuss how animal names are applied to humans, in various languages
4. *Sound feelings* (p.20) Learners explore their reactions to the sounds of various languages
5. *Borrowings* (p.22) Learners explore words borrowed from other languages, by means of a matching exercise
6. *Word-for-word translation* (p.24) Learners translate proverbs from their own language into English

II: Sound–spelling

7. *Form-focused spelling puzzles* (p.30) Learners use crosswords, wordsearches and anagrams to improve spelling
8. *Syllable snap and rhyming snap* (p.33) Learners focus on vowel sounds and syllables by playing card games
9. *Sneaky spelling practice* (p.36) Learners improve spelling while playing games or problem solving
10. *Colour-coded sounds* (p.39) Learners improve sound discrimination by means of colour association
11. *How do I say it?* (p.42) Learners group words according to sound patterns

III: Denotation

12. *The definition game* (p.48) Learners practise defining and understanding definitions by playing communicative games
13. *Tools of the trade* (p.50) Learners review names for objects and occupations by playing a communicative game
14. *Instant recognition* (p.53) Learners discuss contexts for social sight words
15. *Hearing and visualising* (p.56) Learners share personal responses to chosen art works or possessions
16. *Experiencing is knowing* (p.58) Learners use story telling, drama and visualisation to explain abstract words

IV: Word grammar

17. *Compound word stress* (p.64) Learners practise varying stress pattern to alter meaning

X: Vocabulary within written discourse

XI: Vocabulary within spoken discourse

Postscript:

B: Activities by type

C: Activities by language proficiency level

Most activities in this book can be adapted for any level. However, this index indicates activities particularly suited to a given level.

Elementary

Intermediate

Advanced

15W16082

D: Activities by student type

Most activities in this book can be adapted for all types of student. However, this index indicates activities particularly suited to a given student type.

Children

Teenagers

Adult

ESP